Frank J. Scott

The Art of Beautifying Suburban Home Grounds of Small Extend

Illustrated by upward of two hundred plates and engravings of plans for residences and their grounds, of trees and shrubs, and garden embellishments

Frank J. Scott

The Art of Beautifying Suburban Home Grounds of Small Extend
Illustrated by upward of two hundred plates and engravings of plans for residences and their grounds, of trees and shrubs, and garden embellishments

ISBN/EAN: 9783337224301

Printed in Europe, USA, Canada, Australia, Japan

Cover: Foto ©Lupo / pixelio.de

More available books at **www.hansebooks.com**

RETREAT FOR THE UNIONISTS.

EYE-WITNESS;

OR,

Life Scenes in the Old North State,

DEPICTING THE

TRIALS AND SUFFERINGS OF THE UNIONISTS

DURING THE REBELLION.

BY

A. O. W.

"Man is not born *alone* to act, or be
The sole asserter of man's liberty;
But God so shares the gifts of head and heart,
And crowns blest woman with a hero's part."

BOSTON:
B. B. RUSSELL AND COMPANY.
S. S. BOYDEN, CHICAGO, ILL.
1865.

Entered according to Act of Congress, in the year 1865, by
B. B. RUSSELL & COMPANY,
In the Clerk's Office of the District Court for the District of Massachusetts.

Stereotyped and Printed by
J. E. FARWELL AND COMPANY,
37 Congress Street.

DEDICATION.

TO THE FRIENDS OF LIBERTY WHEREVER FOUND.

To GENERALS GRANT, SHERMAN, AND BURNSIDE, AND OTHER OFFICERS OF THE ARMY AND NAVY; ALSO THE SOLDIERS, WHO HAVE SO NOBLY FOUGHT OUR BATTLES:—

My admiration of the devotion you have shown to the cause of preserving the integrity of the Union, the unspeakable joy of receiving from your hands Liberty's Flag, and from your lips her words, "Be free;" and, above all, my confidence in your ability to rekindle, through the length and breadth of my *adopted State*, the signal fires of "76," are my inducements to dedicate this work to you.

The part I bore in the trials and sufferings which form the subject of the following narrative, is my voucher for its authenticity.

PREFACE.

The prevailing opinion at the North is, that there is but little Union feeling at the South, and that of rather an equivocal character. Should these pages be the means of convincing any of our Northern friends that there is a strong, imperishable feeling existing for the Union and "Old Flag," it will compensate in a measure for the trouble in bringing these pages before the public.

This work was mostly written at the South, more than two years ago, while these scenes were being enacted. The incidents here related are true. The characters are drawn from life. The writer was conversant with most all, while others, were related by the actors themselves. Liberty has been taken to weave them so together, as to form a pleasing narrative, and by this means they will reach, and be read, by a greater number, than could be found to read each isolated fact; and this knowledge of the Unionist sufferings would be more generally known, and my promise to those heroic souls in part cancelled.

The question has often been asked, both in public and private, what are the feelings of the Southern women in regard to this war, striking as it does at their homes and domestic relations, uprooting at once their long-cherished and inherent distinction, of mistress and slave. To this part of the community, these pages are chiefly confined. You are taken to their firesides and homes, during one of the greatest struggles ever witnessed by mankind. In this respect, it will be found this work differs almost entirely from all others written on Southern life. The world has never witnessed greater devotion, nobler instincts, and heroic deeds, than has been developed by these uncompromising Unionists. Those brave, self-reliant souls, who have shown such patient endurance, self-denial, and unflinching courage, are worthy of a "niche in the gallery of Fame." In time, it will be admitted that the real heroes and heroines of this war are these Unionist men and women.

How successful this attempt to portray the position and feelings, trials and sufferings, of our friends South, during this lamentable strife, the public will now best judge.

CONTENTS.

Chapter	Page
I.—The Soldiers' Relief Society	9
II.—Two Unionists caught	17
III.—The Power of Gold on the Hunter	24
IV.—A Southern Home	30
V.—The Victory at Big Bethel; its Results	35
VI.—A Friend in Need	38
VII.—Miss Helen relates her Adventures	48
VIII.—A Unionist on Trial	70
IX.—The Swamps a Retreat for Loyalists	78
X.—Presentation of a Flag	83
XI.—A Mistake in a Profession	87
XII.—Family History	93
XIII.—Mother and Daughter, Mistress and Slave	99
XIV.—Escape of Mrs. Weasel; finds a Friend	105
XV.—Dr. Hall, and his Patient	114
XVI.—A Storm, and its Effects	121
XVII.—The Patient and Boy saved	127
XVIII.—Introducing new Characters	131
XIX.—Preparing for the Ball	140
XX.—Ignorance and Hatred	151
XXI.—The Revel—how it ended	155

CONTENTS.

Chapter	Page
XXII. — The Effect of the Fight at Manassas	161
XXIII. — Visitors to the Mineral Springs	165
XXIV. — The Death and Burial of an Officer	169
XXV. — News from Washington	175
XXVI. — Butler Panic	186
XXVII. — Maggie and Ralph	189
XXVIII. — Richard Whedden's Escape	196
XXIX. — Heroism	199
XXX. — Unexpected Friend	213
XXXI. — Scenes in Newbern — the Winter of 1862,	227
XXXII. — The Railroad Bridge on fire	237
XXXIII. — Maggie in Prison — finds a sick Soldier	241
XXXIV. — 13th March, Storming the Forts; 14th, Fall of Newbern	247
XXXV. — The Flight from Newbern to Kinston	252
XXXVI. — Annie McGowan's Letter — A Friend is found	257
XXXVII. — Conclusion	272

EYE-WITNESS:

OR,

LIFE-SCENES IN THE OLD NORTH STATE.

CHAPTER I.

THE SOLDIERS' RELIEF SOCIETY.

That gun!

The city heard — and was soon a "city of stirs."[*]
But not with the privateer and his white-winged
victims, whose arrival that salute heralded, nor with
the exultant crowd which thronged the streets and
landing, to see the Yankee vessels, and their crews,
have we to do at present.

Into a pleasant breakfast-room let me introduce
you, reader, and to its occupants, three, — a gentleman and two ladies. The gentleman is speaking: —

"Then the 'Pigeon' is in? Miss Helen, I must
see your brother. Have Nise at the door in five
minutes," he said, turning to a servant; "you will
go with me."

"Stay, no haste, Mr. Blout. Will has been so
long without sleep, a forty-pounder would not awake

[*] Wilmington N. C.

him. He will be at papa's office at twelve o'clock; finish your breakfast, then take my carriage to town."

"And you will spend the morning with Maggie? I accept your offer, and will bring your brother out with me to dine."

We will follow the ladies to the window, where they had moved, that their conversation might not be overheard.

For some moments Helen Bierce, the early caller, sat absently drawing her gloves through her delicate fingers. Then, raising her head with startling abruptness she exclaimed: —

"Why does not Harry Blout fit out a privateer? he certainly has ample means for doing so. It is unaccountable to me," she added, "how any one can enter the army when such another field for serving the South is open to them. This privateering would suit me splendidly! to secure two such prizes as the 'Pigeon' has just brought in; to meet an *armed turtle;* put on steam, up and away, and, just when the danger of capture is most imminent, slip over the bar, and up the river home! There is no State in the Confederacy like our own for such sport, for none has such a coast, — sand-bar on sand-bar!"

"Harry looks upon privateering as nothing less than piracy upon the high seas," said her companion; "I have heard him say, repeatedly, the luckless fellows, caught in the act, would meet the pirate's doom, and deservedly."

"And I see by your looks, Maggie, you are of the same opinion. However, I have no disposition to enter into a discussion of the legality or illegality of the thing; that is nothing here or there now, so long as it is sanctioned by our President. To change the topic, one object of my visit here this morning, is to secure your services on the morrow, for a begging excursion."

"Do not urge me, Nellie," Maggie replied, with a deprecatory shake of her head; "surely there are others, differently situated from myself, to share your burdens and divide your cares."

"So there are; but none who can aid me so efficiently as you."

"My purse is at your disposal," was the evasive reply.

"Your time would serve me best."

"That you have; look at this pile of military cloth."

"There are willing hands enough for such work; mere machine drudgery. My sorest need is for your personal influence upon the obdurate hearts my eloquence does not affect. Now hear of a recent affair which occurred with one of our merchants, Mr. Weasel, then you can better appreciate some of the trials and annoyances which attend the Visiting Committee. One after another of our ladies called upon him, soliciting aid; Minnie Bent made the first advances, but fled, like a frightened canary, from his most emphatic 'nothing to give.' Others tried, but with no better success; finally, our President, Mrs. Vinton, declared her intention to visit the miser; and did so. Imagine our surprise, when, not an hour after her departure, her carriage returned, piled high with bolts of domestic flannel, yarn, and innumerable other things, of which, for a long time, we had been in desperate want. From Mr. Weasel's store they came, for there was his card attached to the bundles! 'Spirited away they must have been,' we cried, 'for nothing could leave that store without cash down!' and we knew when Mrs. Vinton left us she had not a dollar in her purse. To all of our entreaties to make known her weapon of attack, she smilingly shook her head saying:—

"'Time is money; let Saturday night find this goodly heap made up into garments and packed for Richmond.' At night, when the room was deserted by all but ourselves, she related to me the incidents of the morning's call. But you are laughing, why?"

"Nothing much."

"Mr. Blout cannot hear us?"

"His breakfast and paper seem to engross his attention."

At the name of Mr. Weasel, a close observer could not have failed to notice that the loiterer at the breakfast-table was unusually cautious in setting down his cup, and that his paper remained unread in his hand. Indifferent as the young man was to female chit-chat, Helen, had she noticed it, could not have complained, for that morning at least, of his taking only a negative interest in her conversation. His look of interest and inquiry, however, escaped her, and she chatted on incautiously loud. When Mrs. Vinton's name was mentioned in connection with Mr. Weasel's, an irresistible impulse brought Maggie's head without the folds of the lace drapery which graced the window. Her eye caught Harry's; the significant glance escaped detection, but the unfinished smile brought the question.

Satisfied that Maggie alone heard, Helen resumed:

"I must give you Mrs. Vinton's adventure in her own words: 'I stepped into the store and found Mr. Weasel complacently awaiting customers. I returned his gracious salutation, complimented him upon having so full a stock of goods at such a time, and selected some hundred yards of domestic, — but here are the packages, so I need not particularize. His alacrity in bringing down and putting up his goods, and in sending out for what he had not, was really quite refreshing. The secret is, his many refusals to help fit out our soldiers have aroused the suspicion that, at heart, he is a traitor. Consequently no one goes into his store except those whom necessity drives there.

"'You are purchasing supplies for the soldiers, I perceive, madam,' he remarked, glancing at the huge bundles as he tied on the last string and affixed his card; 'where will you have them sent?'

"To No. 9, two doors this side of the barracks."

"You are a great friend of the soldier."

"Not more than yourself, sir, I hope."

"Not more than I should be, did I see the necessity for arming men."

"Where was there ever a greater?"

"War, Mrs. Vinton, is with us, as yet, but an abstract question."

"I cannot agree with you. The recent fight at Big Bethel shows me this war of independence is fairly inaugurated, — a war, which may prove unprecedented in its expenditure of treasure and kindred blood, but one, which shall see the South *free* or blotted out of existence."

"The fight at Big Bethel, madam, was a mere skirmish. A few more such, and some conciliatory measures will be adopted, and then an end put to this strife, ruinous alike to North and South."

"This is a time for action, not argument, Mr. Weasel. Willing hands must work if we would follow up our successes." Then, seeing that I was deliberately drawing on my gloves, he said: —

"Excuse me. At any other time we should be happy to have your name on our books, but now" —

"No apology, sir. I have no desire to have it there."

"You see," said he, pointing to a white card above his head, on which two very black words were painted, "'My terms are cash.' Something very scarce, very precious, just now."

"But not so precious as the blood, that has been already and is to be spilled before we can call ourselves free from Northern rule, Northern cupidity, Northern fanaticism. When this struggle is over, when you have found your security in the brave soldiers, who do battle for you, for all; if this cash-account is not wiped out by blood, generously spilt, by suffering patiently borne; then, sir, I will sell my own flesh and blood to Northern vandals and cancel your claim with their villainous gold."

"All very well, madam; all very well! but I have no use for any body's flesh and blood. I demand my money!"

Not noticing his interruption, I continued — "When the call came for three hundred thousand men, our people uprose nobly. Who was ignoble, cowardly enough to think of the *pay* he should get! Ours is a common cause; the old and infirm stay at home: they give freely, give all they possess; the young and brave fight, women and children work.

Cash down! Money! Serve your country, sir! imitate the example so nobly set by your countrymen, and your one talent of money-making shall be as blest to you as the five talents profitably laid out by the wise servant in the parable," and I turned to leave the store.

"Zounds! madam," I heard; "flesh and blood can't stand this! — it is theft, burglary of high order! — restore my goods, or, madam, you shall feel the full rigor of the law!" As I reached the door, Mr. Weasel was at my side; Pete, however, at my order, had driven on. I left him in his store door gazing after the carriage, crying — "too late! too late!" Now, Maggie, was n't that well done?"

"No, Nellie, your own true sense of justice tells you Mr. Weasel was right, when he said 'such a procedure was burglary of a high order.' Let those give who do so willingly, not ——"

"Nonsense! Maggie," interrupted Helen, "you remember the old adage, 'the end, if a laudable one, justifies the means;' and if to put the screws on misers, to make them disgorge some of their ill-gotten gains, is not justifiable, it is, at least, *merciful;* for we spare these money-changers, these 'votaries of Mammon,' the horrible fate of falling a sacrifice to their own devotions, by lopping off shoots of interest, as we would the boughs of a tree, breaking beneath the weight of its own fruit, — is it not so? But let me finish my story: the week's close found our work complete, and the box packed and marked — 'Soldiers' Relief Society, Richmond.' It was left in the work-room, the door was locked and every window secured, — I am sure of that. Monday morning, when Pete went to the building, the box was there, but not a shirt, comfort, sock, blanket, or bandage, — no not one, to be seen! Of course the negroes are accused of the theft; but Mrs. Vinton and myself have discussed the matter thoroughly, and, having heard nothing from the belligerent gentleman of Store No. 70, are convinced that to catch a *weasel* asleep is no easy matter. We, however, shall match him yet; for let the public be fully assured that this Mr. Weasel is one of the proscribed set, Union men, and not one box-ful but his entire stock is ours."

CHAPTER II.

TWO UNIONISTS CAUGHT.

An unusual noise from without, at this moment, attracted the attention of Maggie and her guest, and fully conscious that the tumult was approaching the house, they arose and through the open window stepped on to the verandah. As the curtain fell behind the retreating figure of her mistress, Lizzie from her lookout groaned: "It makes my blood freeze to har dem hounds; somebody's blood runin' when dey howl like dat!" Then dropping her work and herself upon her knees, she prayed that the poor, hunted negro might find favor in the sight of the Lord, who made him, and be spared the torture of his white master.

"Confound that —— —— of an abolitionist, — see how he bleeds! Swing him from yonder limb, or he'll die before we twist the necklace! He'll fight for Old Abe, and nobody else — will he? Swing him, and let him try his strength with them buzzards yonder! Hear 'em cracking their beaks! — hold on a bit, old fellows, the meat will soon swing!" Such shouts rent the air as, mounted and afoot, an eager crowd pressed round their victim — a man not more than twenty-five, and a boy scarce eighteen; whose clothes, if such rags might so be called, were mired and fearfully rent, displaying the gaping wounds where the bloodhounds had taken hold.

Deadly pale, but undaunted, the man walked in the midst of his merciless tormentors, seemingly unconscious of his own sufferings, though the warm blood trickled from his legs and shoulder, where the burnt flesh showed only too plainly, the nearness of the weapon, the sure lodgment of a ball, which had buried itself in his broad chest.

No persecuted runaway negro was he, kind reader, but worse, far worse, — a hunted, hounded, and denounced "traitor"! — the victim of an enraged and maddened people. His crime, the oath to stand by the good old flag, and Abe Lincoln, forever!

Again and again the prisoner turns a fond and encouraging look towards the sinking boy at his side, who, faint with loss of blood, staggers on, now pitched forward by a kick from behind, then sinking from sheer exhaustion amid the feet of the crowd; while large drops of sweat, mingling with the tears, his agony wrung from him, poured down his face and bloodstained body. Human nature could bear no more. The fierce grapple of the hounds, the kicks and oaths of the exultant captors, were now alike unheard, unfelt.

As the stalwart hunter's arm was upraised, bearing aloft the lash, now of a deep red dye, which told of the strength of its cruel owner, a cry went out from the bloodless lips of the brother so heart-rending that for a moment the slave-driver was cowered and his arm fell to his side.

Fiercely his victim tugged at the iron bands, which bound his hands before him. The flesh parted and the blood flowed at each endeavor, but the iron would not give; deeper and deeper it sunk into his flesh; it was not felt, but in his soul it rankled and tore.

Must the boy die thus? if life was still there, must the last lingering spark be crushed out beneath the trampling hoofs of the horses, whose merciless riders jeered and mocked at the misery they caused? Could these be men, with hearts of flesh, who could so wantonly kill and so derisively laugh at that one, last look for mercy; mercy, not for himself, but for the dying, innocent boy, who lay at their feet?

Yes, they were men: made after God's image, rich in acres of cotton lands, and turpentine lots; boastful of many heads of negroes; pleasure-seekers; livers in the saddle; *not drunk*, the day was not far spent enough for that; not wholly soulless nor heartless, for there were *those* in that crowd, so eagerly thirsting for blood, so jubilant over the death-agony of their victims, who had voluntarily encountered peril of fire and water to save human life.

To plunge into the swollen creek amid the pitiless storm, which had overtaken him, to rescue a drunken, worthless fellow, whose stumbling steps had slipped from the foot-logs; to bear him on his back to a distant cabin, to find it deserted, and then walk the night out in a soaking rain to secure aid for the dying wretch;— to dash amid the burning ruins of a cabin and bring to the widowed mother, her missing boy; to drive from sight the overseer for brutally beating the "boys," because not up to the task assigned them, — were deeds, done from the natural promptings of these very hearts, which now madly yearned for the lifeblood of a Yankee sympathizer, — the "traitor," who would sell his countrymen into the most galling of all vassalage — that to Yankee lords!

Once more the fair listeners on the verandah shuddered, as that wild, agonizing cry reached them, and — pitying heaven.

A powerful arm upraised the boy; and an eye, which flashed the challenge that struggled for utterance upon his lips, repelled the crowd.

Athletic in figure, his large, black eyes dilated and flashing, his face a-glow with the honest anger which burned within him at the cowardly, dastardly act, just perpetrated, — a perfect type of manly and powerful beauty, Harry Blout stood, as unconscious of the deference which, on being recognized, was obsequiously tendered, as of the sun which beat scorchingly upon his uncovered head. He bent down, and lifting the bleeding body handed it carefully to a servant, who had followed him to the road.

"There is life yet," he said, placing his hand upon the boy's heart; "take him, Pomp, to Aunt Lizzie. Bring water," he added, "and a sponge; hold, bring brandy, your mistress will tell you where it is to be found."

The crowd, speechless, heard these orders given, nor was a hand raised to prevent their execution; for know, reader, that these men in soldierly array were a company of Blout's Rifles, proud and boastful of the name they bore, splendidly equipped as was the entire regiment of which this company was a part, by the munificence of the one whose presence held them spellbound.

What wonder is it that they spurred their horses from the road, and, seemingly engaged in managing their suddenly restless steeds, endeavored to escape the withering look which was turned upon them. But the fierce, hang-dog eye of Grimes, the hunter, brightened as he recognized the man at his side; for even this brute, rich in the possession of the fiercest pack of bloodhounds to be found the country around, who spent six days out of seven in the woods and swamps, starving his "pets" to fatten them upon the blood of the luckless runaways, whom they never failed to scent and fasten themselves upon, had heard of and seen the city wonder, "the Cuban cousin;" upon whom was showered exuberant praise, such as "rich as Crœsus;" "generous as handsome," "such munificence princely revenues alone could support;" and the like.

"Never did a better chance offer to make good his losses," (in the morning's scuffle, two of his hounds had been killed,) he said, in an aside to one of the crowd, and the natural repulsiveness of his brutal face was heightened by the smile which the comforting words called up. At a stern gesture of command, the handcuffs were struck from the lacerated wrists of the prisoner, his wounds cleansed, and his weary frame invigorated with stimulants. Then, for the first time, turning to the hunter, Harry Blout demanded the price set upon the boy's head.

"No price," growled the man, the scowl which the question brought increasing as the unwelcome truth was drawn from him.

"How came he in your power?"

"Caught him with that d—— abolitionist yonder," pointing to the man whom Pomp, at the command of his master, had mounted upon his favorite saddle-nag.

"Why let your dogs take his life?" Harry asked

sternly. At the savage answer, Harry turned away and beckoned Captain Green, who, for a commissioned officer had, on this occasion, been refreshingly modest, to approach.

"This is your first appearance with your company," he said; "I congratulate you upon the occasion which has so heroically displayed the courage of the men in your charge. Take this man," he added, the sarcasm in his voice giving place to command, "into your care, and see to it that he is spared further abuse until, at least, he is in the hands of the city authorities."

Captain Green bowed and gave the order for his company to form. With remarkable alacrity they wheeled their horses into line, and, with the prisoner, slowly paced down the road.

Swindled into Secession by as diabolical a fraud as could be perpetrated; straining every nerve to fill her quota of troops; suffering her noble-hearted sons to be denounced and imprisoned because suspicion marked *them* as "traitors." Stricken, convulsed, torn, pouring out her treasures of blood and gold into a tyrant's lap, to be scorned and publicly maligned by him, as weak, cowardly, a drag upon the Young Confederacy, *North Carolina*, — where these scenes are laid, — lay wrecked and helpless, — the victim of South Carolina's treachery and Virginia's bold, unscrupulous, law-defying partisans. Who that is conversant with her mighty struggles to break from her bleeding hands the manacles of iron despotism, could doubt, had she been situated as Maryland, Kentucky, and Missouri, that as many of *her* sons would have emptied their veins for the preservation of the Union, as those States can boast?

Up to this time no executions had defamed the once fair name of the "staid old State." That lynch-law was to be the order of the day was apparent to all.

CHAPTER III.

THE POWER OF GOLD ON THE HUNTER.

SIMULTANEOUSLY with the departure of Captain Green and his company, Harry Blout turned to the slave-hunter. He was stooping low in the road, vainly endeavoring to staunch the blood which flowed from the side of one of his "pets," whose lolling tongue, dull eye, and gaping wounds, tell of a fierce struggle within, — a struggle which will never be repeated. Even now he falls upon his side, and with imploring eye begs for the caress his master bestows with a lavish hand; his eyes close, his jaw drops; nothing but the slowly wagging tail tells of his gratitude. Big tears roll down the fierce-visaged man's cheeks, for he knows his dog must die, — yes, is dead already. With a wild stare and a convulsive tremor of the bleeding body, a third victim of the morning's hunt has been offered upon the altar of human rage and demoniac fury.

Fire flashed from the hunter's eye as he turned upon the one who stood by, an unmoved spectator of the scene; and curses thick and fast rushed to his lips, but were checked as he noticed the cool, determined face turned towards him. A low voice met his ear bidding him name his price for the remaining hounds, — would he sell? There was but a momentary hesitation. The negro-hunter worshipped his profession and his hounds, and he as devotedly worshipped the gains they brought, and to sell his dogs was to throw himself quite out of employment. Comforting himself, however, with the thought that with the handsome sum, such as he should demand, there were other fields where his talents might have full scope, he signified his consent to dispose of his pack. With the price named he growled, "not too much; give 'em blood — "

With a gesture of disgust, Harry silenced further encomiums upon the "pets," and handed the man the amount he asked; then, with a significant glance, bidding Pomp "take care of the dogs," he cleared the low gate with a leap and entered the house.

For such as Grimes, war was a profitable thing. Never was heard such a running away of negroes; and with the tales of bloody violence and vicious theft which followed, came the unceasing cry for "hunters and bloodhounds."

But a degree of danger attended these hunts, — for not a limited number, but scores, hundreds of runaways infested the woods and swamps, which made even the boldest of them tremble for their lives and their dogs, when the scent was struck and the grapple at hand with a dozen or more stalwart negroes, who had scented the blow which was to waft them to liberty.

Hunters were not infrequently found dead beside their dogs, and such negroes, as were brought in, were but few in number, and, in most cases, crippled for life. The pay, therefore, although fair, scarcely compensated for the risk.

So it followed that nine of ten of these followers of the negro-hunt disposed of their packs to the more venturesome, and stood in the ranks as substitutes,— their services being purchased by such lukewarm partisans as cried " war! war!" and then, with glass and pipe, settled down to the comforting reflection that war, on the whole, was a good thing; for, if productive of no other result, it swept the streets of paupers, and city and country of a " rake-helly" set, that lent themselves to be the instruments of any villainy, provided the pay were good.

In the prevision of the ardent antagonist, however, there was no such inglorious end to a strife of which they were the abettors and supporters, but a free and recognized South. *One red field*, one thunder-like groan from a prostrate, suppliant foe, and a people had attained their pre-ordained position, — that of framing for themselves a new, bright destiny.

But to the few, uncorrupted, undaunted defenders of Unity and Law, that " first gun at Sumter" was no signal-gun, arousing a people, oppressed, to rise and burst the shackles of despotic power. To *them*, *that gun* was a death-knell, booming over the South, bidding " Chivalry" rise and finish the work, defeated ambition and unextinguishable rancor and jealousy had begun, — *the digging of their own graves!*

Having carefully chained his pack of hounds, Pomp followed on his master's footsteps. He stopped not at the house, but over the lawn, by the stables, down through the orchard, he trudged; his eye flashing the intensity of his joy, which the proper time and place heard to roll out, peal after peal, from the very depths of his capacious chest.

Seeking the shelter of a wide-spreading gum-tree, he stopped to rest, and, holding his hounds at arm's length, thus soliloquized : —

"Oh! Massa Harry, dis yer earth has no other like yer; neber did dis yer old boy tink to be de massa o' sich a pack o' devils own imps! 'Pears like de good Lord knows I'se de man for dis 'ticular case; for wid his 'mission, ye old sinners, ebery one o' ye shall be dead 'fore mornin' breaks."

The dogs yelled and tugged for freedom, as though in the eye of their keeper they read the doom which was to be theirs before the advent of a new day.

Up and on, Pomp toiled; his cabin is reached at length. With a kick the door flew wide, and the glad cry which followed effectually silenced his yelping prize. So did it also "Robert O'Lincoln," who from a neighboring tree looked with his mate the surprise he did not utter, then alighted upon the window-sill of that usually silent abode and curiously twisted his bright head to see his old friend, the exultant possessor of such a dog-prize, so uproarious.

But, for a moment only did that dark form, stretched upon the floor of his sanctum, give utterance to his exuberant joy, for work was to be done. With the agility of youth he sprang to his feet, and in a twinkling a staple was driven into a log and the dogs chained fast to it.

One long, lingering look he fixed upon the snarling, fighting creatures before him, then turned and left them.

Duty calls Pomp to the "big house;" ours is not so imperative; so we will linger awhile in his cabin.

It had been built by his own hands, and, what was Pomp's delight to tell, was furnished by his young mistress. The hard, pine floor, white as soap and sand could make it, the three rough but strong chairs, a mirror and a couch, bespeak nicety and ease; and the clay pipe and long reed stems, show no neglect. The bed with its white spread occupies one corner of the room, and at the foot of it, into one of the logs of the cabin, Pomp had driven the staple and confined the hounds. Fox and coon skins adorn the walls, interspersed with a rare collection of birds. These, we see so carefully stuffed and tastefully arranged, were not brought down by *his* barrel; boys would kill, and Pomp would expostulate but all to no purpose. Silently he would creep to the hedge, where the ruthless hand had thrown a bird, and when no care could restore life, he would stuff and cherish its beauty, as if a pet of his own raising.

If we lift the huge skin, which hangs at the foot of the bed, we are in possession of a secret, — Pomp's long-cherished secret, which, for him, has *Paradise* in it.

One look will suffice. Under its soft, secure shelter is a high-colored picture, bought of a pedler, prized beyond all earthly treasure, because descriptive of the equality of all men and of *freedom's* day.

Christmas after Christmas, the day of their redemption, as Pomp and his race fondly and fully believed, came and went; but not that one which was to see their chains undone. The great Emancipator still tarried! Neither faithless nor discouraged, but all believing, they bent their backs for another year's burden, and patiently suffered the chains which the Lord could lift up and cast off when he should awake to the miseries of his afflicted children. Pomp was no " Uncle Tom," for teaching his brethren patience to await the Lord's coming; but those who saw with how much resignation he toiled on from day to day, faithfully and thoroughly obedient in discharging his manifold duties, could not but respect and honor him. There was a time when he pined so for freedom, that his little mistress, her father's pride, took pity on him; and, with childhood's winsome ways, sought to overcome her father's obdurate will. But this is all that came of her earnest entreaty:—

"My darling daughter, grieve me not by asking what would bring misery, the most abject, upon Pomp. Dry your tears. Pomp's life is a happy one; he has all he needs; lays up money yearly; is cared for, well housed; fed and clothed. No, no, my child, papa knows what is for Pomp's good, and will always shield him from want and harm."

"But, Papa, you will die one day," the child would reply, "then Pomp shall be free, for I will make him so."

"Not so fast, little heiress. Papa will have to make a will, which shall restrict his wayward darling;" and he would add, pressing her to his heart, "all generosity, all love. God grant my life may be spared to shield you from the ills poor black Pomp would so blindly rush into."

CHAPTER IV.

A SOUTHERN HOME.

WITHIN the suburbs of the city of ——, our story leads us. Just far enough removed from the busy hum and din of city life, stands a noble mansion, decorated by the hand of taste in possession of an ample fortune.

Broad and sweeping lawns; gigantic trees inviting repose beneath their vine-clad, out-reaching arms; garden plots, teeming with the luxuriant products of that sunny clime, interspersed with exotics from other countries; a rich, dark belt of forest trees encircling the grounds on the north and west, — lent an irresistible charm to this beautiful home.

The house, built of brick, is of almost palatial dimensions. Light and graceful verandas adorn the front and sides; here the white scented jasmine wanders in unrestrained luxuriance, clinging to and completely covering the light columns, curtaining windows, and over-topping the broad, flat roof, wraps the high chimneys in a green and deliciously fragrant mantle.

Nor had the taste of the owner confined itself to outward adorning. The lofty rooms glow with the creations of genius. Splendid portraits, pictures rich in historic lore, and charming landscapes grace the walls; while statutes, statuettes, busts, and gems of rare value are artistically arranged throughout the rooms and broad halls.

John Blout, the noble and fortunate possessor of this delightful abode, enjoyed a high social and political position.

A West Point graduate, his powerful intellect, ready wit, and rare personal qualities gained for him, not only the highest honors of his class, but the unbounded and outspoken admiration of his associates, North and in his own State.

To make his State illustrious, not by extending its limits and multiplying its slaves, but by the diffusion of knowledge, so that the natural resources of his native soil might be developed; and her sons ("how like to the rudeness of their dear native mountains") might bring to light, polish, and exhibit "the rich ore in their bosoms,"—was the thought which warmed his heart and stimulated his mighty soul to almost Herculean efforts. But when his cherished schemes gave promise of speedy fruition and incalculable good, the thread of life parted!

The grief of the household was most profound; and the wail of the orphan was echoed by many a sympathizing heart, which bowed and wept for a benefactor gone.

A favorite brother had long been a resident of Havana. The only issue of his marriage with a rich and noble Spanish lady was a son, who had just reached manhood, when the devoted wife and most exemplary mother was removed by a sudden death from their loving embrace.

In foreign travel, father and son sought to divert their minds from the excessive grief which bore so crushingly upon them.

Three years spent on the Continent and in Asia, found the wanderers homeward bound.

Amid the splendors of court-circles; amid the inexhaustible stores of priceless treasures which the old world seductively displayed to the cultivated mind and artistic taste of the travellers, both felt the same irresistible yearning for their beautiful, but shadowed home.

On arriving in their own sunny clime amid the congratulations of friends, the news of the brother's sudden death, and the sad entreaty of the orphan that her uncle and cousin should share her desolate home, came, and admitted of no delay.

They embarked the day but one following their arrival home, for the " States."

Only two days out, the vessel which bore them encountered a terrific gale. Though staunch and strong, the waves engulfed her; she went down, and all on board perished, save one, who was picked up by the ship Champion, on her way in port. Strapped to the survivor was the dead body of the father, both being lashed to a plank.

By the unwearied exertions of the officers of the Champion, the young man's life was restored; but so grief smitten he sat by the box which contained his father's remains, that the noble-hearted men around him forbore to question, seemingly satisfied with the brief intelligence, that the Sea Gull, from Havana, foundered at sea in the late gale. Crew and passengers had probably gone down in her, as the boats were stove at every attempt to launch.

Richly rewarding the humane captain and crew for their noble exertions, in his behalf, Harry Blout, once more on shore, sought his island home, and, with his own hands, laid the loved parent by the hallowed remains of his mother.

Before the fate of the Sea Gull had been publicly announced, Harry was again on board ship, hurrying to offer to his stricken cousin the sympathy which his own sad heart yearned for.

Long years before, he had visited his uncle's family with his parents. Well he remembered his great and good kinsman; his warm-hearted, loving aunt; whose death followed their departure South; and his charming cousin, Maggie, the pride and pet of the household; a rare bud, giving promise of perfect womanhood.

And "woman's coronal of triple graces, beauty, modesty, and truth" never graced a nobler brow, or a more gentle and generous nature. Subsequent events proved, that underneath that mild and courteous manner, was a strength of purpose and an indomitable will, which the consciousness of right could alone make her to exercise, and no persuasion, however seductive, could move. Though the idol of a large circle of devoted friends, no sympathy was so grateful, no care, no society so soothing, so unobtrusive, and withal so congenial, as her cousin Harry's.

Proud she well might be of him. Handsome, chivalrous, frank, and generous, his was a heart animated by powerful human sympathies; his a courage defiant even of death.

Both cousins were rich, sole heir and heiress of their parents' unbounded wealth.

To free her negroes, to put into their hands the means of obtaining an honorable living, was Maggie's long-cherished and ardent wish; and, during the sad year which followed her bereavement, many plans were projected for their enfranchisement. With her cousin's invaluable aid, legal steps had been taken for their freedom; a tract of land negotiated for, and men engaged to carry out her most humane project, — when the principles of a Southern " Revolution" were whispered of, and soon were fully afloat.

It is impossible to conceive of a more agitated and violent state of society. Fathers, sons, brothers, friends, fled homes —

> " The resort
> Of love, of joy, of peace, and plenty, where,
> Supporting and supported, polished friends,
> And dear relations mingle into bliss—."

and, shoulder to shoulder, stood in hostile ranks, wildly and maniacally shouting, "War!" Many, alas! confident that some compromise would be effected, held back, until neutrality could no longer be tolerated. Then there was no choice, but to take up arms in defence of the infant league, or languish in a felon's cell.

A fearful ordeal for the loyal soul! — but many a one there was, who, scorning the traitor's livery, fell a martyr to the holy cause of Liberty. The world may never know these martyred heroes, but, on high, in the " Eternal Book," their noble deeds are recorded, written by the " pen of truth."

CHAPTER V.

THE VICTORY AT BIG BETHEL — ITS RESULTS.

Shouts of victory rent the air, making the dark night of despair and treachery tuneful, when tidings were sent along the lines of the telegraphic wires, of a complete and overwhelming victory!

The first onset of the foe at Big Bethel had proved, what the popular cry had again and again reiterated — "that all Yankees, debased by abject and menial occupations, were cowards, constitutionally."

"O! Maggie," cried a merry Rebel bursting in upon the cousin's revery, their hearts wrung by the news the morning's paper announced, — "What a splendid victory! and so cheaply won! the cowardly Yankees did not stand the first round of shot! away they all 'flew like the down of a thistle,' when General Hill gave the word, 'Up! boys, and at them!'"

"I have read the particulars of the fight in the morning's *Post*. We certainly got the better of them. There was one brave soul there, however, we all can but admire."

"Yes, *one*, who took a fair look at Dixie boys. Brother James was near him when he fell. I have his letter with me. Shall I read you what he wrote of him?"

Maggie eagerly assented, and the young girl opened her letter and read:—

"There was one Yankee officer, and but one, Sallie, who stopped to fight us. Deserted by his men, he stood bare-headed shouting to the cowards to turn and charge. I would as soon have shot myself as that brave fellow, and, although within a few yards of our guns, not a soul was there in our regiment that would raise an arm to bring him down; fired with admiration, as we all were, at such intrepid courage. Creeping up from behind a cedar thicket, one of our men would have held him prisoner, in five minutes more, when a shot from a hut near pierced his heart. A rush to the spot, and there was that miserable John Cobb, boasting of having brought one high buck down. If Col. Hoit had not been in the hut, it would have gone hard with the scamp. Hoit said, pointing to the body, lifeless as the log by which he fell, 'Look to it boys, that the Yankee yonder does not beat you in the fight, which was in him. Stand firm as he stood, face to a rain of lead, and this hour's victory shall crown every struggle with Northern Vandals!'"

"The *Post* says it was Col. Corcoran, of the Seventh New York."

"Yes, Maggie. One paper says Col. Winthrop,[*] and another asserts it was some one else; all give him praise for heroic efforts, worthy a better cause. There is not another so courageous a soul North, I know; had he been on our side, fighting for his home and all he held dear, what a hero for us to lament."

The signal victory of June tenth gave a most

---

[*] It was Col. W.

momentous impetus to the cause, which the boldest had at first tremblingly espoused. Fired by the enthusiasm which victory can alone incite, proudly confident that one more such inglorious defeat would settle the " fuss," and the let-alone principle be a compulsory affair on the part of the North, innumerable hosts rushed to the field. Every exertion was made, every effort put forth to equip the inhabiters of village, town, and city for the impending struggle at Manassas — " the grand finale of this most unnatural contest." Days and nights were spent in unremitting toil. Stores closed,— not for repairs or lack of custom, but from the stubborn fact that there was nothing to sell — were searched and researched for some little article, which had escaped the eyes of the party detailed for begging and indiscriminate store sweeping. Private dwellings were up-turned and out-turned of every available comfort, so clamorous was the cry — " more, more," from camp, barrack, and field. Blankets were cheerfully snatched from beds, soon to yield sheets and pillows for the hospital sick; the shirt, which was worn to-day, was on the morrow cleansed and stripped for bandages or scraped for lint; while the music of the knitting-needle was stunning to ears refined.

The giving was noble, the sacrifice nothing, for, said these self-devoted patriots, " Before the cold winds of winter shall rock the pines and whistle through the cane-brake, Old Abe's ships will be rotting in Northern harbors; while free trade, the great monopolizer and deadly foe to Northern commerce, will fill, yes glut, the markets, which the horrid, barbarous, exhausting blockade has brought to a distressingly collapsed state."

CHAPTER VI.

A FRIEND IN NEED.

THE morning of the hunt — the one made mention of in the opening chapter of our narrative — a gentleman sat on a broad veranda, seemingly engrossed by his cigar and newspaper. His pet hounds tumbled and tossed at his feet, intent upon the demolition of the Panama hat, which their master had thrown aside, that the wind might cool his brow, now contracted and severe as his eye scanned the telegraphic news of the previous evening and the comments of the press.

With a contemptuous sneer he tossed the *Examiner* from him, and with agitated steps paced the veranda.

"Egregious fools!" he sharply uttered — "to preach 'peaceable Secession,' and when that foul bubble exploded, to hoodwink the masses with such abominable trash as 'cotton is king,' 'foreign intervention.' England and France will not, dare not to intermeddle. Commercial gain is no fair match for such principles as they boast. 'For humanity's sake!' — yes, when the North and South are torn, despoiled of all power, exhausted as they surely will be if this war goes on, these transatlantic vampires will show their humanity in the cry — 'every man for himself,' as they pounce down upon us to batten upon the spoils of a disrupted nation."

"The North can whip us if she bares her arm for the blow, and nothing remains for the South but annihilation, and extermination of every man, woman, and child. They have brought it upon themselves; let retributive justice be meted out to them, full measure, pressed down, running over, — *they deserve it !*"

Resuming his cigar, Richard Whedden for a moment eyed the nearly demolished hat, then picked it up, flung it on his head and sauntered down a broad walk, which through a noble growth of trees, led to the road.

A noise from below growing louder, he stopped, and leaning carelessly against a huge live oak, was, to a chance observer, an indifferent spectator of the brutal treatment which, farther up the road, was so humanely stayed.

Scarcely was the crowd by, when a long, shrill whistle brought to the master's side a black-skinned, chubby little fellow, who, hat in hand, with eyes and face aglow with fun, stood demurely awaiting the coming order: "My horse, Cars. Three minutes, not a second over to bring him here," fell upon the ears of the fast-retreating figure, who, leaping, tumbling, and shouting "Dixie Land," sped on until the "lot" was reached. Not "three minutes" but twenty found Mr. Whedden seated on a noble bay, slowly cantering up the road.

He drew rein at Maggie Blout's gate. "Is the boy dead?" said a strong and manly voice at her side, as Maggie, with her hands full, sprang from a porch, up a low flight of stairs, which led to the room where the wounded boy had been carried. Too intent upon her mission of mercy to notice the strange tone; delighted to have some one near to relieve her hands, that she might fill them anew, she exclaimed, without turning her head, "Take these bottles, I have forgotten the camphor. No, no. I will see the boy,—here, take my keys and go to the buffet and bring the camphor bottle. Quick! now. The poor boy's life depends on our despatch." In her eagerness her keys became entangled and would not yield to her nervous fingers. "Unbuckle my belt and the keys will fall," she said impatiently. "Dear, dear, you are so slow!"

"Pardon me, madam, I am not accustomed to buckles," was the quiet reply. Eager as Maggie was to reach the sick-room, there was something in the voice of the speaker which made her turn to look. With one glance over her shoulder, down fell the bottles from her hands outstretched to save the fall which her overwhelming confusion threatened. Too late! but strong arms caught and placed her upon the narrow step now moistened with laudanum and ether. This was no time for apologies — none were expected.

"I am seeking the sick boy," the stranger said, "one of your servants told me I should find him at the head of these stairs. Shall I take the remaining bottles up with me, or seek the camphor?" he asked with a scarcely perceptible smile.

"Take the bottles, if you please; it is the room at the right," said Maggie, and with a light bound she cleared the glass-strewn steps and entered the house.

The long hour which had elapsed since Maggie left her side, was spent by Helen Bierce alone in the parlor. Deep emotion, which pride had repressed while there were those near to witness it, now wholly overcame her; and, as with agitated steps she walked the long room, large, scalding tears, such as never before had stained her haughty but expressive face, rolled down upon her bosom.

"Why don't Maggie come?" at last escaped her; "I will tell her all." Then wrapped in her own troubled thoughts, she murmured — "I cannot appear as that man's accuser. How nobly he risked his life to save mine! how tenderly he bore me in his arms to his mother's door! how kind his voice and his eyes — foolish, foolish girl!" she cried, springing once more to her feet, (for she had thrown herself upon a couch to stifle her sobs in its cushions,) — "can this be Helen Bierce, thus to yield to tears and womanish pity! To my country's need I have pledged my energies, my life. God grant if it be mine to seal a traitor's doom, that this heart, these ears of flesh may be turned to stone!"

Not long, and Helen stood once more on the veranda, no trace of her recent emotion visible except in her heightened color and the unusual brilliancy of her eyes.

Her attention was shortly attracted to her coachman, who was untying a horse at the gate.

"Whose horse is that? Jim," she cried.

"Dun know, missis, neber see'd him afore," the boy said, as at a motion of his mistress, he led the curvetting steed to the spot where she stood.

"He is indeed a superb creature," said Helen, attempting to pat his arching neck; "don't you know to whom he belongs, Jim? why it is not more than a week ago, I heard you tell your master you knew *everything*, when urging him to take you to Virginia with him."

"Thort I did, missis; but you've cotched me in a tight place dis yer time. Beg pardon, missis. I hab it. Massa Whedden rides him. Dun know nother such beauty de country round."

"Who? Mr. Whedden down yonder?"

"Yees, missis."

"Not so, Jim; for Mr. Whedden never comes here. Do you question the servants —"

"No need o' dat, missis," said Jim, interrrupting, "its my 'pinion dat he owns dis yer horse hisself, and nobody else."

"Jim, I tell you this horse does not belong to Mr. Whedden. Here is an opportunity to make good Dine's loss. Have him I must; a thousand dollars would be well invested in such a prize. Take this," she said, tossing her servant a bit of paper, a substitute for money, "and do you, Jim, seek the owner and make known to him my wish to purchase his horse."

Again bending forward she attempted to stroke the creature's glossy mane, but desisted at length warned by the dangerous proximity of one of the small feet, that his was a nature decidedly unapproachable.

On re-entering the parlor she met Maggie who, relieved somewhat by the physician's words, "there is an even chance," had left the sick-room.

"Well, Maggie, you have come at last," she exclaimed, drawing to her side, "how weary you look. Why so overtax your strength when you have a house full of servants?" Then without waiting for a reply she asked abruptly, turning her head that

Maggie might not read the eagerness which her face expressed: " Will the boy live?"

" We hope so. There is an uttter prostration from loss of blood. Dr. Bell says had the wounds been neglected until medical aid was secured, he could not have lived the day out. How thoughtful in you to send me his mother's address." As Helen made no reply, she resumed : " How my heart aches for this afflicted mother; her life seems bound up in her sons. Harry spoke with her shortly after her arrival, and she seemed much relieved when he promised her to see Charley (as she calls the elder,) before night. 'To know the brother was in his mother's care,' she said, 'would nerve him for the terrible ordeal before him.'"

" Maggie," said Helen, while a sudden whiteness overspread her face, " I have a sad tale to tell you, but not now, you must rest first."

" Nay, tell it to me now. This fatigue will soon wear off — and your story may serve to banish the fearful scene of this morning."

A deep, heart-felt sigh escaped Helen; but recovering herself, in a light tone she said, — " If talking will ease you, do tell me who that gentleman is who owns so matchless a horse, and what brought him here to-day? The horse is just such a one as brother Will wants, and has been the State over to find. Poor Dine, he says he shall never make her loss good."

" Dine dead! Nellie, when did that happen?"

Waiving her question, as through the half-open door she saw Harry Blout approaching, with forced gayety Helen pressed her inquiries concerning the stranger: —

"You saw him, Maggie?"

"Yes."

"Where?"

"In Aunt Lizzie's room."

"Then he was the physician whom you called in?"

"No, but he bound up the boy's lacerated limbs; indeed he took every thing into his own hands, Harry and myself only acting under orders, so quietly and promptly given one would imagine he was a regular practitioner."

"But you have not given me his name."

"The stranger was none other than Richard Whedden, our nearest neighbor."

"Impossible!" exclaimed Helen, in unaffected amaze, — "Do you know that churl?"

"I have seen Mr. Whedden pass the house often, but have never met him until to-day."

"And this, his first call here, was in an old nigger's room, binding up the wounds of a boy picked from the street!"

"Why not?" said Maggie, rebukingly, — "such suffering as we have witnessed to-day would move any heart not of insensate rock."

"Yes, I suppose so," Helen made answer, somewhat abstractedly. "But you have met him before?" she added, turning to Harry, who had entered the parlor, and seated himself near the cousins.

"Yes, Miss Helen, in Europe."

"Anywhere else?"

"In Washington, last March."

"*He*, certainly did not go on to the inauguration of that Western Rail Splitter?"

"He is not a man to be questioned as to his motives, Miss Helen."

"No, I suppose not. I was North when Mr. Whedden made his appearance in this neighborhood; but even after my return, some months subsequent to his advent here, his name and oddities were the theme of many busy tongues. And do you know no more of him, Mr. Blout, than the world about here knows?"

"My acquaintance with Mr. Whedden is recent, and withal, slight," — said Harry.

"You have been at his house?"

"Occasionally."

"Every thing in and about the house bespeaks refined taste and wealth, I am told."

"Yes."

"Strange," said Helen, musingly, "but from the slight glance I had of his face, as he passed down the lawn with you, some moments since, I was forcibly reminded of our illustrious General, Arthur Whedden." As her remark elicited no comment, Helen resumed — "And bearing the same name, I am almost convinced, that what has been but vaguely surmised may have the correctness of truth."

"What is that?" asked Harry.

Maggie shook her head deprecatingly at the questioner, and, before Helen could make answer, said: —

"You speak of a likeness between the two. Where did you ever see General Whedden, Nellie?"

"Some years ago, while travelling North, an accident threw Mr. and Mrs. Whedden into our party. We learned they were from Charleston, and pleasure-seekers like ourselves. Beauty, wealth, and talent of a high order, set off by most polished manners, lent a charm to these strangers, which was quite irresistible."

"Charlestonians!" said Harry, sententiously.

"Laughing at me, both of you, for rhapsodizing these people," was the rejoinder. "I deserve it, however," Helen added, "for no one in days past has ridiculed the aristocratic pretensions of our semi-royal neighbors more than myself. But I speak what I know to be wholly true, when I say, that the merit of these two Charlestonians cannot be overestimated. True nobility of soul is recognizable——"

"When covered by the purple robe becomingly worn," interrupted Maggie, laughingly.

"And we may expect," chimed in Harry, "if, in the course of events, Richard Whedden claims kin to General Whedden, he will also be entitled to a share of your admiration."

"When he has shown himself worthy of it, yes," said Helen, with some hauteur.

"And if one, blest with the power of divining the occult, should point out a general's star in Richard Whedden's destiny, eclipsing the one worn by——"

"Richard Whadden a general! *he*, the embodied essence of selfishness, never! Men of his class, men who ignore all social and religious ties, I fully believe are but the vagaries of nature, wholly heartless and spiritless, possessing not one of the noble attributes which grace the statesman or general."

"Thoroughly used up," said Harry, oracularly, as he turned away, too generous to let Helen see the merriment her words occasioned.

"Be not so uncharitable, Nellie," said her cousin, gently. "The kindness shown to a stranger this morning by Mr. Whedden, coupled with like acts with which I am conversant, convince me that some sunbeam yet may penetrate this armour of haughty reserve and chilling seclusiveness, and find a heart exquisite at the core." The door, at this moment, was thrown open, and Mr. Whedden was announced.

The gentlemen soon left; urgent business calling them to town. Hardly were they out of hearing of Helen's voice, when she exclaimed —

"Maggie, he must be kin to Arthur Whedden; if they were brothers they could not look more like. Come to the window," she cried, springing up. "There they go down the road. See how he sits his horse — horse and rider as one — a noble centaur!"

"What further rhapsodies will the name of Whedden call forth?" asked Maggie, as she arose and joined Helen at the open casement.

CHAPTER VII.

MISS HELEN RELATES HER ADVENTURES.

The calm hour of eventide found Maggie looking out into the gathering darkness for the return of Harry, that she might bear tidings of the prisoner to the trembling watchers under her roof. At her side Helen still lingered, striving to nerve herself to the task of unburdening her heart, a heart whose better impulses were being uprooted fast by stern war's hateful bane. Winding her arm caressingly about Maggie, as they sat side by side, she said at length, — "Hear what I must tell you, and then strengthen me for what I must do."

Little did Helen think, that the one, to whom she turned for support, for courage to crush the *woman*, so she might serve her cause, was of the tabooed set. — Yankee sympathizers. Maggie's seeming indifference to the exigencies of the hour was attributed to the great shock she had sustained in the death of her father. Selfish, as many thought her, to allow her bereavement to make her so unmindful of her country's need, no thought, no suspicion of the truth that she was intensely *Northern* in her proclivities, was entertained. And Maggie Blout was but one of the many who said, "our forces," "our successes;" who looked grave, and smiled unwillingly, when shouts for "Dixie" rose; and who refused to contradict powerful telegrams, which sounded, "Yankees whipped," "armies completely demoralized," "peace suing," &c. &c. To make known their sentiments was not only to restrict the little good a limited sphere could effect, but doom themselves to imprisonment, to atrocities, the human heart shudders to chronicle. They knew the irresistible power of *right*, and they felt that right must ultimately prevail.

"What troubles you, Nellie? tell me," Maggie said.

"You know, of course," Helen replied, "that all of our city ladies, except a few like yourself, who from family troubles have not met with us, have bound themselves by a vow as sacred as mortals can utter, to aid the South in this unnatural strife. My trial has come, and finds me weak, vacillating, and wretched." "Your trial come, you have had it with you since these troubles begun," said Maggie, as Helen stopped and turned away her face in the vain endeavor to recover composure.

"No matter what I have done, it is what I have to do, which makes me tremble. First, hear this," she added, taking a note from her pocket, "it was sent here some hours since, then I can tell you all:—

MY DEAR DAUGHTER: That miserable Coxe has been caught at last. Instead of visiting summary punishment upon the traitor, he is to have a hearing to-morrow. Dr. Hall is out of town, consequently your testimony alone convicts him. Return to-night; you go to the court-house to-morrow. I thank heaven my daughter is brave to do her duty.

Your loving father,
F. BIERCE.

"Nellie," burst from her cousin's lips at the conclusion of the letter, "it cannot be that you——" she stopped, then added, "this is very sad, but tell me all."

"It is soon told. Not long since, on one of my begging excursions, the horses took fright as Jim was dismounting to open the carriage door. They dashed down Danforth and Green streets on to Main, and were within a few feet of the railroad track, as the cars came in sight. A terrible doom awaited me, but at this critical moment, a man on horseback leaped at the horses' heads. With a blow Dine fell to the ground. I sprung from the carriage; I was calm, much more so than I am now, but, in jumping, I caught my dress, and was thrown with great violence against some timber near the track. I was not wholly stunned, for I remember being picked up and borne by strong arms some distance. After hours of unconsciousness, I awoke to find myself on a bed in a strange house; at my side sat a dear little girl, sobbing bitterly. Voices from an adjoining room met my ear. I listened, thinking I might get some clue to the people who had so kindly befriended me; and I heard, 'Mother, do leave me. The sick lady may revive and need your assistance.'"

"I must attend to you now, Charley; I have done all for the lady that my limited skill allows. The doctor, I hope, will soon be here. Dear! this is a bad wound; the flesh is laid open to the bone."

"Never mind, a few stitches will make that all right; I suffer most in my hand. Bathe it once more, then leave me."

"The words were scarcely uttered when a heavy fall and a stifled groan assured me I was not the greatest sufferer. What a dear, brave woman that mother was! She came softly to my bedside. 'I am glad,' she said, 'that the lady is still unconscious' Winnie, your brother has fainted. I cannot wait for Dr. Hall, I must go for some other physician. Don't be afraid, but be a faithful nurse, I shall soon be home.'

"'Won't the stranger cry when she wakes up and sees all this blood?'

"'No, no, kiss me good by, and remember to keep very quiet.'

"How long those moments seemed! I thought no longer of my own pain, I thought only of the brave soul near, faint from anguish. Not long, and a low voice called from the room beyond the one where I lay. Softly as a kitten Winnie stole away, and again I was a listener.

"'Has she spoken yet, Sis?' I heard.

"'No, Charley, but oh! she is so white! maybe she won't wake no more.'

"'Is mother with her?'

"'No, mamma has gone for a doctor.'

"'Why, George went long ago.'

"'Mamma went right off when you fell down. What made you, Charley? you shook the house awful.'

"'Why, little one, I did not go down purposely. But, tell me, were you with mother when she dressed her wounds?'

"'Yes, mamma and me did them up.'

"'What could such little fingers as yours do?'

"'Oh! I took off her slippers, and her stockings, and her ——'

"'Never mind what she had on, Sis. Tell where she was hurt.'

"'On her head, and there is a great hole in her shoulder, and her bosom is all red. Won't she be cross with mamma for cutting her clothes so?'

"'No, not when she knows it could not be helped. Go in to her room now, and see if she still keeps so very still; and mind, if she is conscious, and wants anything, come and let me know.'

"'On tip-toe she stole in and up on to the bed. When she saw my eyes open, she would have jumped down, but I held her fast. She told me her name was Winnie Coxe. 'Are you all well now?' she asked, 'and can Charley do anything for you; he wants to——'

"'First, tell me who Charley is?'

"'Why, Charley is the one who stopped the horses; yes, and he brought you way here in his arms. Don't you suppose they ached some? mamma says, you are right smart fat.'

"'He was very brave and good, certainly. Did the horses hurt him?'

"'Yes, he got hurt awful, but he did n't make one bit of fuss. He said he would n't mind being most killed for such a pretty lady.'

"A noise in the next room took the little nurse away, to see what kitty had knocked down. She came back directly, but spoke not a word, and only shook her head when I asked her what mischief pussy had done. Dr. Hall came in soon afterward. He was, I thought, remarkably quiet. He examined my cuts and bruises, and said in the morning I could be carried home. Mrs. Coxe and a stranger, whom I afterwards learned was Dr. Brown, came in at this time, and seeing me in Dr. Hall's care, passed into the next room. I begged Dr. Hall to follow, that I might know just how badly the young man was hurt. He did so, and came back to me saying: 'A kick from one of the horses had injured one knee very seriously, and one hand and arm were in a badly inflamed state.' The doctor left, after seeing me comfortably arranged for the night, and promised to call at the house to quiet all apprehension on my account. Papa, I knew, would come directly to me and bring Kizzie, which would relieve these kind strangers from nursing me longer. I fell asleep, and on awaking was conscious that it was night. A murmur of voices from the room adjoining met my ear. I would not listen, but lay studying why no one came to me from home. The voices grew louder. I heard papa's name mentioned, and that alone fixed my attention. This is the conversation, which, with startling distinctness, came to me:—

" 'What a confounded affair this, just as we are off, Charley! We shall put off our tramp to Liberty's land, however, until you can go with us.'

" 'You are mad to speak of delay, Bill. You must start by to-morrow's dawn, as agreed upon.'

" 'What, leave you here to don old Jeff's' livery or swing?'

" 'Yes. I must now take my chance alone; but if shut in here *forever*, no earthly power shall make me lend a hand to the most diabolical conspiracy which ever was hatched, or spill Yankee blood,— so help me God.

" 'Yes, yes, Coxe, we know the temper of the steel you are made of, and we boys know, too, you are the very one for the Rebels to clutch. Your name was handled roughly enough to-day; but we, who were in the secret, laughed inly, you may be sure, for we knew that another sun would find us all in the mountains. By St. Peter! I would rather have lost my chance of getting out of the State altogether, than to see you thus crippled.'

"'I would like to see the boys before they 're off, Bill.'

"'Never fear, not a soul of the gang but will lay eyes on you before they set out.'

"'What came off at the Court House to-day, Smith, — any more secesh speeches?'

"'Secesh speeches, — yes! Bierce was holding forth as I drew up. I tell you what, Dr. Brown, the "old line whigs" have n't a greater enemy in the State than he.'

"'Confound him! If it was n't for Hattie's sake I'd rid the earth of such a monster. Coxe, if it should get to his ears that you are of the tabooed set, Yankee sympathizers, there's death ahead sure. He's a keen, killing shot, and handles a bowie knife as a schoolmaster his pen.'

"'That may be, Brown; but I have no fear of meeting him.'

"'Better not, Charley. Shun him as you would "black Jack." He's not a man to forget an injury; the sins of the fathers upon the children is the creed he lives up to.'

"'Enough of that, Smith. See how it worries the man.'

"'Well, Brown, Bierce will not find a disciple in you; that's so, if you do swear you 're secesh out and out.'

"'Yes, boys, for my wife's sake and my child's I swear I'm secesh, and curse Abe Lincoln till my

tongue is as black as the souls of these d——
Breckites! Had I no family I'd cut profession,
niggers, everything I own here, and strip for Liberty's run. My ——! what a glorious pull-up
there is in store for you!'

"Steps upon the walk I now heard, and many
feet passed into the house. Low voices uttered
regret at their friend's mishap, and many offers were
made to await his convalescence, that his might not
be a lone journey to Uncle Sam's pastures. All
were, however, firmly but kindly refused. Adieux
followed, and the crowd silently stole away, the
doctor alone remaining.

"'Lincoln won't put weapons into those boys'
hands for nothing, Coxe. If they don't show what
fight there is in them, they'll deserve the fate which
awaits them if caught. But tell me how they are to
get out of this d—— Confederacy?'

"'They are to strike different roads to Salem;
there they are to meet and push on together for the
mountains. Once in the defiles of the Blue Ridge,
with liberty to cheer them, and Kentucky is theirs!'

"''T is a mean thing, old fellow, that you must
lie here bed-ridden and lose this glorious chance.
If I could put my valuables into a sack for my back
I'd set off to-night.'

"'Your wife and child might object to that mode
of travel.'

"'Hattie, never! She'd go through fire and
water to reach her former home; and I would, for
her, to get her safely there.'

"'Is she from the North?'

"'From Pennsylvania.'

"'But you can get a pass for her and child from
Gov. Ellis.'

"'Ellis, why he's a dead man, or what's more to the point, soon will be.'

"'Clark succeeds him. What sort of a Governor will he make?'

"'Clark! he's a senseless fellow.

> "His wits were given him for a token,
> But in the carriage cracked and broken."

By the way, Coxe, what smash-up was it which brought you on to your back?'

"'I paid no heed to the carriage, for the lady demanded all my attention.'

"'What was done with her?'

"'I brought her here. You remember Dr. Hall gave me a call shortly after your arrival.'

"'He came to see her, did he, and carried her to her friends?'

"'If I remember rightly she was not to be moved until morning.'

"'Where in thunder is she, — not in this house? Why, man, what's the matter? you are shaking like an ague subject.'

"'There is cause for some alarm, Brown. It has just occurred to me that this evening's conversation may have been overheard by this stranger.'

"'There's mischief ahead, Coxe, as I am a living man.'

"'She may be sleeping.'

"'True; I'll soon convince myself of that fact, however. If she shows the least consciousness, — hang the match! it won't light, — I'll—'

"The remainder of the sentence, in my extreme agitation, I lost. Conscious that I was unknown, and that my life, perhaps, depended upon my remaining so, to escape from the house was my only alternative. But how to effect it! each moment was precious, for escape I must, before Dr. Brown could bring his candle to my face. I was confident he would recognize me; for, from the moment of his mentioning his wife's name, *I knew him*, — knew him as a man apparently of strong secesh proclivities. Now his life was in my hands; the knowledge of that alone I felt would make him desperate. Steps were approaching; my resolution was taken. I sprung from the bed and behind the door through which he was to pass. As he crossed its sill and advanced a step beyond it, I waved my handkerchief; the sickly, flickering flame went out. With an oath he turned back for another match, and I heard him curse the night air for serving him such a trick. The door, which opened upon the veranda, was ajar; on a chair near it I remembered seeing Mrs. Coxe, on entering, lay her shawl. It was but the work of a moment to throw it over my head and reach the street. Swiftly I ran until I gained the railroad track, then stopped to take breath. From the house which I had left a light streamed out, whose beams revealed a group looking out into the night for a delirious sick woman, as no doubt they thought me. The clatter of hoofs, coming thick and fast, compelled me to leave my point of observation and seek the friendly shelter of a culvert. *Horresco referens!* the rider drew rein as he reached the spot where I crouched. Closer I gathered my scant garments about me, and sunk deeper into the muddy water. The horseman leaped to the ground. He must have seen me, I thought; I placed my hand over my mouth and laid my length in the dark stream. He sprung down the bank, — 'Fool that I am,' I heard, 'I thought I saw something white. Ah! there's the carriage yonder; that will perhaps give me some clue to the missing woman.' Up the steep bank he climbed; I was safe! I raised myself and crept half way up the embankment, and by the faint starlight saw my pursuer examining the carriage. Baffled there! I could have shouted; for the carriage was a new one, and I knew the light was insufficient for him to recognize Dine. 'Thank heaven for murky skies! I shall escape you yet!' I mentally exclaimed. But no, his attention is again attracted towards me. Could the winds have borne my unspoken words to him, or did my eyes, which glared upon him, draw him towards me by some mesmeric power! Hateful thought! I closed them and my mouth firmly, lest my fierce breathing should betray me. Towards me he came, slowly; one foot actually crushing the twigs which lay by my side! One moment of intense emotion, and then I breathed freely. Oh! what a thanksgiving swelled my heart when I saw the man mount, and heard the clatter of his horse's hoofs down the road!

"When I again reached the track the city clocks rung out one; the day had already begun. As I neared the city, desperation and the horror of detection nerved me to almost superhuman exertions. Elm and Green streets were finally reached and safely too; the night-watch were not over vigilant; I saw, but escaped them. On Danforth, one more square, and I should reach home! alas! a boisterous crowd suddenly burst upon me. Providentially St. Luke's Church was at hand. I had time only to reach the friendly shelter of an arch, when the men swept by,

— officers and privates of our regiment on their way from the hall. How my heart leaped when I heard brother Will's voice! (he was urging on a man, who had lain down upon the church steps, declaring he would sleep the night out there) — and it made me strong to encounter further peril. The two finally moved on, and I glided away. In a few moments I stood upon our balcony. I knew where Will's night-key hung; it turned in the lock, the door opened and I stole to my room. I lighted the gas; then walked to the mirror. One glance sufficed: that Dr. Hall must be sent for was as evident as the necessity of my removing every sign of the direful disorder of my appearance before ringing for aid. When the light of the coming day first streaked the horizon my task was complete. I rung for my maid; the cook answered my summons. I told her I was sick; that Dr. Hall must be sent for; and that Jim must come directly to my room. To satisfy my own curiosity as to the absence of so many of the family, she told me on entering that papa had been called out of town and had taken his wife and Kizzie with him. I must expose myself to the like, and I was determined that no one should know of that night's adventure but our good friend and physician, Dr. Hall, for in his judgment and keen sagacity I have the most implicit confidence. Jim came to my room; and of him I learned, that, in attempting to follow the carriage, he had fallen, and, although much hurt, had managed to crawl home. In his uncommon fright, he said, he was waiting for his master to come in to make known the accident, when Dr. Hall drove up. He told him I was safe, where the carriage was to be found, and bade him go for me in the morning. Dine he had ordered shot; she was so crippled by her fall. To my inquiry, why he (Jim) had not sent for the carriage, he said, 'he set the boys off for the live horse, but he thought dead property might go until morning.' I told him I would give him one hour to bring home the carriage, and dispose of Dine; that if he was not up to time I should report him to his master, and he knew what would follow. He moved quickly away, utterly regardless of the night's bruises, if one he had; and I heard him mutter, as he closed the door,—'don't 'gree wid young missis to git upsot; neber seed her look so like old missis afore.'

"How impatiently I waited for the doctor; I felt I was sinking, and did so need my maid to nurse me. It was the first time papa's wife had carried her selfishness so far as to monopolize one of my servants; and the want of Kizzie, at this time, made me feel more thoroughly angry towards the woman, who fills my mother's place, than any of her acts of petty tyranny, daily practised upon one and all of our household, had ever done.

"With my head upon the window-sill, I watched for that well-known buggy; I saw it drive up; then a strange giddiness seized me. Recovering myself, I found Dr. Hall at my bedside. My first question made him laugh outright. 'I did not strike you, wilful girl,' he said. 'I came here at your bidding, and receiving no answer to my knock at your door, I opened it and found an empty bed. A shape, enveloped in a window curtain, however, attracted my attention; I picked it up and find it has a tongue.' He scolded me well for risking my life to secure home nursing; but not until he had bound up my arm anew and had administered an anodyne would he sig-

nify his consent to hear what I had to tell him. Of
my nocturnal adventure I told him all; not one word
of the conversation which I had overheard escaped
me. Very grave, he sat, and I even heard him sigh
as I finished my recital. How my heart blessed him,
when he said, 'Helen, leave all to me; I will answer
all inquiries, solve all mystery, and keep your secret.'
And, Maggie, at my earnest solicitation, he promised
to aid the young man, traitor though he is, to escape
from the State. When I remarked, that Dr. Brown
should be exposed, he said: 'He was a former student of mine; but leave this affair wholly in my
hands; you certainly can trust me.' With the promise to report to me what success he might meet with,
and that his delay should be as short as possible, he
left me. A severe run of fever followed that night
of fright, exposure, and fatigue. When I awoke to
consciousness, I found Dr. Hall in attendance. Of
him I learned that, on leaving me, that memorable
morning, he had gone directly to Mrs. Coxe's house.
He found the family in great anxiety, concerning my
mysterious disappearance, but quieted all their apprehensions, without exciting a suspicion of the real
cause of my flight. Dr. Brown, he said, was not to be
found, and, giving up the search for him, he returned
to the house to find me alarmingly ill. To papa, he
had explained the accident, and the cause which had
occasioned my flight from the house where I had been
removed after my fall. He avoided giving papa the
name of the people who had befriended me, but said,
in the delirium of fever I not only mentioned their
name, but aroused his suspicion as to their character.
He told me also, that papa had made inquiries with
regard to them, and was now only waiting my con-

valescence to ascertain of me if they were correct. And he added: 'the young man, Helen, is beyond pursuit, — I have done your bidding; now take my counsel and have no words with your father on this subject for several days to come.'

"What I told papa on the following day more than satisfied him that Dr. Brown was a traitor, and for him, we both agreed, there was no doom too ignominious. When he mentioned my preserver, I pleaded headache; that a few days would find me sufficiently strong to tell him all that followed my fall. Considerate, as he usually is, he seemed deeply to regret the delay I urged, and said : ' You spoke the name of Coxe. I know of but one family of that name in town. It may be, yes it may be, that my memory has played me false.'

"'What may be?' I asked.

"'That this Yankee Brown's boon companion is John Coxe's son.' To my inquiry who John Coxe was, he replied —

"'A bitter, bitter enemy of mine, Helen; a man of some talent, but low-born, and possessing little wealth; a man the world would never have known had he not allowed himself to become the willing tool of the Whig party. Twice was he elected to the Senate. Not a Democrat among us, however, but was conversant with the frauds practised to secure his election; but, my daughter, men like your father, gentlemen by ancestral rank, and possessing all the advantages which wealth and intellect command, step back from the strife and permit high places to be polluted by such miscreants as the Whig party gives birth to, rather than suffer personal contact, or the altercation which must follow, where aristocratic supremacy is assailed by plebeian animosity. That man's assumption, however, cost him his life; he fell, pierced to the heart by the assassin's knife, while canvassing the State for a third election. A young man of that name, I hear, has lately appeared at the bar. If he is a son of John Coxe — (I lost all knowledge of his family some years ago) — and proves to be the one we seek; I say, if he is Coxe's son, and possesses but a shadow of the dogged obstinacy which characterized the old man in the support of his party, — (a party, thank God, we have throttled), — yes, with one word, that in him Abe Lincoln has a minion, and his doom is sure!'

"At night papa came again to my room. He and his men had been to Dr. Brown's, but their search there was fruitless. I needed not to ask of the other, for his look confirmed my worst fears. 'Not caught,' he said to my mute appeal; 'but John Coxe's son, he is!'

"'How did you know where to seek him?' I faltered.

"'Jim directed us. I saw the mother; when the mob surrounded her house she stepped out on the veranda; there, white, but self-possessed and dignified, she stood, amid the execrations of my baffled men. To their demands she said: "God gave, and to his care I have resigned my son." "Three days ago I saw him leave this house with your son George," was shouted from the crowd. To the threat that her house should be fired if she persisted in her obstinate silence regarding his place of concealment, she replied: "Fire my house, rob me of all I have, but never will I utter one word which

shall betray my boy into the hands of lawless men!"
I did not stay to see the threat of the mob executed.
The defeat, which I had twice sustained through
John Coxe's agency, Helen, was fully cancelled by
the sight of the suffering his folly had entailed upon
his family. As I drove up Danforth Street, the
flames of the burning buildings lit up the sky; and
to the eager ears of the many, who leaned from
windows and balconies to question,—the reply, "A
Yankee conflagration!" was received with clapping
of hands and peals of laughter; while "Good! give
us another! burn them all out!" fell from coral lips
and souls loyal and devoted.'

"That night, under cover of darkness, Kizzie
sought the afflicted mother and found her and the little Winnie in a tumble-down negro hut. Not a friend,
if one she had, not a neighbor dared aid or comfort;
nor can we blame them, Maggie, for they knew that
by so doing, they would subject themselves to like
treatment. The basket, which Kizzie had filled for
her, she gratefully took; but it was only after much
entreaty, that she would consent to accept the sum
the purse contained. On leaving, she handed Kizzie
a slip of wrapping paper, on which was written:
'The prayer of the poor and afflicted has been heard
and answered; God has made you the almoner of His
giving. No enemy can stay the prayer of supplication on its way to God; daily shall that prayer be
offered for your welfare, that strength may be given
you to do His bidding. Your maid says you have
no name to-night. In that land, where all ills are
forgotten, I shall joyfully meet and bless, as I do
now, my dear, unknown benefactress.'

"Days went by and nothing was heard of the

runaways; but the scene of this morning has brought back vividly the suffering of that wretched week. I saw the prisoner, Maggie, and prayed from my inmost soul that it might be Dr. Brown. But when my eye fell upon the boy at his side, I knew the doomed one was Charles Coxe!

"I have told you all. Speak now, dear cousin, and teach me how to act, that I may best reach the standard I have marked out for myself."

"Helen," said her companion, with solemn earnestness; "imagine yourself in the situation of this mother, sitting by the bedside of a son just snatched from death's grasp, and fearing that any hour may be freighted with the death agony of another; then tell me how *you* would feel towards one, who with outstretched hand could save, yet passed by on the other side?"

"For heaven's sake, Maggie, do not appeal to my feelings," was the passionate response. "Duty, stern duty, must be uppermost in my thoughts."

"Is the call more imperative now than it was when you besought Dr. Hall's aid to assist this man out of the State?"

"I was sick then," Helen pleaded, "and allowed my heart to pervert my judgment; I have not now that excuse for iniquitous faltering, when the path of duty lies open before me."

"Cannot you leave the sword of justice in the Great Avenger's hand?"

"But my vow. I may not falsify my oath."

"If it conflicts with Christian duty, in our Father's sight, it is better broken than kept."

"Then, Maggie, tell me what *to do!* I go to confront this man to-morrow."

"Do as you would, if your brother, not Charles Coxe, had fallen into the hands of merciless harpies," was the firm rejoinder.

"But we must not forget this man is a traitor, and for all such there is a special reckoning, a special doom," persisted Helen.

"Cousin Helen, is it for us to pass judgment upon a human soul? Are you or I accountable for any one's sins but our own? Look at this matter calmly, search your heart to the bottom, then ask yourself if you dare assume the responsibility of launching an immortal spirit into eternity."

"Still, duty is omnipotent, and if conscientiously discharged——"

"Hold! cousin. Here I hold out Justice's scales and Mercy's curtain. Were sentence to be passed upon you to-morrow, which would your guilty, trembling soul crave?"

A servant at this moment entered and announced the carriage for Miss Helen. As the cousins parted upon the steps, Maggie whispered: "Seek the throne of grace, lay your troubled thoughts there, Nellie, and to-morrow your heart, purified by prayer, shall prompt your words."

"Not here," said Harry, drawing Maggie out of the night-dews (for at the sound of steps upon the walk, she had left the house, heedless of damp and darkness, to relieve her intensely anxious thoughts,) and seating himself by her side on a bamboo settee in the hall, he resumed: "Yes, there is one, and but one hope of young Coxe's escape from being lynched."

"What is that?" gasped Maggie.

"The seizure of the babbler; we've men on his track; if we catch him, Coxe is safe."

"And you have no suspicion who he is?"

"There are a dozen rumors afloat, but with not a shadow of reasonableness in them. I'm off again in a half-hour; let him cross my path!——"

"Harry, I can save you and your friends a night's ride; for I know that the prisoner's fate hangs upon a woman's tongue."

"Then he'll swing!" burst in passionate vehemence from the young man's lips. "Women have gone mad! not one breathes, but gloats ——"

"Hush! dear Harry," said Maggie, laying her hand gently upon his lips, "there are some true women left, and the heart of his accuser, though warped by evil surroundings, is not, I can convince you, wholly corrupt."

"Maggie, you are the exception to all womankind; but in the kindness of your heart you allow yourself to be most egregiously fooled. Aside from yourself and this man's mother, there is not a woman in this city but would cheer on the fiends in their hellish work of swinging up Union men."

"Harry I never heard you speak so passionately before; wait until to-morrow, and, if I have been fooled, as you call it, I will turn Sister of Charity at once, and hide my simpleness in virtuous deeds."

"There, Maggie, don't be vexed; credulity, in a compound sense, shall not banish you from my heart or sight," said he, affectionately drawing her to his side. "Tell me all you know, and make me believe, *if you can*, in a secesh woman's clemency; but stay, I will first tell you my story. Charles Coxe is the name of the young man so villanously used; his father was one of the most successful lawyers and politicians in your State. Among the Union men young Coxe has many friends, and some one of them may speak in his behalf to-morrow, although to do so is to bring upon himself the suspicion of loyalty to the Federal Government."

"Did you go to his cell?" asked Maggie, somewhat impatiently.

"Yes, Mr. Whedden and myself were smuggled in."

"I feared prison doors might be shut too fast for even you to undo."

"Maggie, I never saw iron yet, which would not yield to gold."

"And you saw and spoke with him? Tell me all he said."

"He told us frankly, that, had it not been for an accident, he should have fled the State at least two weeks ago; he was warned he was suspected of being an abolitionist, and left a sick-bed for a hiding-place in Black Swamp. His brother George went with him. In their flight they came up with a negro; of him they learned that two days' journey would bring them to a 'jump and run,' where there was a gum-tree in which was a hollow large enough to hold them both until pursuit was given up. They were within a few miles of the spot, when the baying of hounds told them their tracks were scented. There was then no escape; they told the negro to run; he, however had sheep-skin on his feet and did not fear the dogs, and stayed by until he had armed them both with cudgels. Coxe said, the sight of the bloodhounds roused the strength of a maniac within him; he had killed two, and could have finished the pack had not a shot brought him down. Before he could rise, men were upon him, who ironed and marched him off. He said he did not suffer physically, but he was maddened at the sight of the treatment visited upon his brother.

"We stayed in that loathsome cell some hours; bound up his wounds, which had been shamefully neglected, and left him much comforted and with some slight assurance, that life, and, what he valued far more, liberty might yet be his."

"You told him his mother was with George?"

"Yes. The first words he spoke, when the prison doors swung to behind us, were, 'My brother!' He is the most unselfish person I ever met with. When assured of his brother's ultimate recovery and of his mother's being with him, had the irons been struck from his wrists and his prison bars unloosed by Abe Lincoln himself, he could hardly have been more overjoyed. Now, Maggie, tell me what you know of his accuser."

CHAPTER VIII.

A UNIONIST ON TRIAL.

JULY 7th rose clear and calm, but the sun's rays beat down scorchingly; and although "Lazy Lawrence" could be plainly seen in the dry, parched atmosphere, — a sign for all but workers to stay within doors, — the streets were thronged. Fair-faced women, forgetful of tan and burn, pressed hurriedly on under umbrellas, borne by Afric's dark sons, or languidly reclined in cushioned carriages, fanned by spruce-looking quadroon maids, as perfect in feature, and but a few shades darker, than their proud mistresses; while lawyers, forgetful of briefs, and doctors of patients, with well-to-do merchants, planters, and boys, swelled the crowd, thronging towards the Court House. The doors turn slowly on their hinges and the eager press surges through, flooding the wide entrance and filling the spacious hall to overflowing. Seats were reserved for ladies, but many a bold look and undisguised sneer fell upon the dear creatures, who, with immense efforts, were trying to bring within prescribed limits fabulous folds of muslin and astonishingly refractory hoops.

"No place for women," growls graybeard, just bowed out of a chair by a Miss of fourteen summers.

"I reckon you are right," was the quick rejoinder; "did any one ever see the like of this,—only a three-legged, crazy-back chair to hold me for two long hours!"

"You, Molly, take care! another such a sit down and we shall be floored!" cries a distressed voice. Miss Miffit, white with apprehension, had been watching her plump neighbor, who, overcome with the compound jostle of the crowd, dropped with two hundred pounds' weight upon the creaking bench. The catastrophe of being brought to the floor was for the time averted, much to the relief of the timorous few who occupied the same tottering support.

We will turn from the crowd to look at the prisoner. Disfigured by wounds, pale and emaciated, but fearless, Charles Coxe stood before his judges. He had broad shoulders, a bold heart, and a loyal soul; to die for liberty was indelibly stamped upon his expressive face. From him we will glance at his accuser, Helen Bierce; for it was her name, which, connected with the man's arrest, had filled so many seats with the city's fluttering fair.

At the question, "If she had ever *seen* the prisoner, Charles Coxe?" she raised her lustrous black eyes to his face. Their looks met. Calmly she scanned his features; except a slight twitching of the muscles of the mouth and an increased pallor of the face beneath such searching scrutiny, no emotion was visible: the preserver and the rescued, the suffering but undaunted victim, the high-born aristocratic belle, the loyal soul and traitor's dupe, alike the gaze of the crowd stood unmoved, unread, save by the eye which searcheth all hearts.

Helen turned to the questioner; her answer was a firm, clear "No!"

. Down came the hammer in the hand of brief authority to command silence, for a disappointed mob was growing unpleasantly demonstrative. In the same shrill voice came the question, "Do you know aught of this Charles Coxe?"

"Only what I have learned since his arrest," was the slow reply.

Mr. Francis Bierce, one of the number before whose tribunal the "traitor" was arraigned, then arose. A smile broke over his face, so self-satisfied and bland that, as it met the ladies upon his right, saddened under the unfavorable turn Helen's replies had given to the affair, it carried full assurance with it.

"My daughter, state fully what befell you June 18th."

The eager earnestness of the crowd increased as Helen related what she had previously told her father; but at her concluding words — "that the prisoner in your midst and the man who bore me to that rendezvous of traitors is one and the same, you have no proof, no valid testimony, only a negro's word," — the crowd became uproarious, and, for a time, resisted all attempts to be quelled.

Amid the din Mr. Bierce stood, frantically beating the air in the vain endeavor to call attention to his words. Those near him heard, — "The renegade Yankee Brown has escaped us! but see to it that no more of the vile scum slips through our fingers! Charles Coxe is a Yankee sympathizer, my word for it! Let summary punishment be visited upon all such!"

With the cries, "Up with him! Swing him high!" violent hands were laid upon the prisoner;

RICHARD WHIDDEN SPEAKING FOR THE UNION.

but a powerful man near dashed the ruffian to the floor, with the cry, "Hear, hear!"

That any man should imperil his life by speaking in behalf of the doomed one, awed the crowd; and in their tumultuous eagerness to swell the list of "Yanks" to swing, the greater part shouted, "Who are you? Spout ahead Yankee!" stifling the weaker cries, "String them both up!—no speeches, no prayers for traitors!"

"Who am I?" shouted the bold man; "I am Richard Whedden of South Carolina, brother of your General, Arthur Whedden."

A wild burst of enthusiasm greeted this avowal, for the name of Whedden was a household word. Men forgot the diabolical act which was to imbrue their hands in a brother's blood; and women, unmindful of flies and gnats, dropped their fans, and gazed admiringly upon the towering form, that had gained the *estrade*, and, proudly erect, stood thereon.

Curiosity to hear one who claimed the name of Whedden, his noble enthusiasm and bold speech at first, kept unbroken silence.

To set forth the iniquity of their leaders, custom had taught them to reverence, who declared, when Northern democracy could no longer be made available by the South for the control of the Government, that the South must try the dissolution of that Government, and the diabolical schemes entered into to accomplish the same; to explode the foul bubble, that the North, rather than give up the benefits of the Union, would recall her armed bands and unite with the South under such a constitution as *she* should prescribe; to portray vividly the ruin, which, as a desolating spirit, would lay waste the land from the

Atlantic to the Pacific, from the Lakes to the Gulf, should civil war be fairly inaugurated; to compare the immense naval and land forces which the North could command, to their own limited numbers, crippled finances and lack of resource; to depict the desolation which must follow the tramp of reckless soldiers through fields ripe for the sickle and cotton-picker; through cities flourishing, and those, too, which had lost their bustle, but not their pride, left to be sacked and burned, while old men, women, and children, fled from the outrages of brutal soldiers to the mountain fastnesses, or buried themselves in pestilent haunted swamps, was the subject-matter of his harangue.

The shaft of truth sunk deep; and, when the impassioned speaker ceased, its effects upon that homogeneous throng, where all the elements of riot were so fully developed, far exceeded his own and his supporters' most sanguine expectations.

True, he had often been interrupted by the muttering of the storm, which threatened, but which was kept under by the many, whose better natures had been aroused, and who clamorously shouted, "More! more!" With the glow still upon his face, which warmed his heart, that his words had not been uttered in vain, Richard Whedden once more arose, and, after a powerful appeal to their feelings in behalf of the prisoner, said, "I told you I was a South Carolinian; my ancestors died in defence of that soil. Once I was proud of my birthright; but, if to be a South Carolinian means a nullifier, a seceder, a traitor, an insulter of the proudest flag which ever swept the ocean wave, or floated upon liberty's embattled heights, I renounce my State now and forever! and, if God wills, I will be the first to quench the flame she has kindled to fire the South! If to be a Yankee sympathizer means a lover of the Union and of the Constitution (the only one which the South can be safe under), a fearless defender of Columbia's flag, I glory in the name, and will die in defence of the honor that proud title awards me!"

"Die, then!" shouted a voice from the crowd.

The whistle of a bullet followed, and Richard Whedden staggered, but was caught by friendly arms.

That shot was the keynote of the voluntary which followed. Riot of the fiercest kind prevailed; shot fell thick and fast, and, amid oaths, groans, the whistling of bullets, and the crashing of glass, the shrieks of women rose wild and shrill. More and more desperate grew the deadly affray. Pistols were dropped, and "Down with Secesh!" "Death to the Yankees!" hand to hand the rioters engaged. Those at the windows were calling loudly for aid, when a crash, as if the building was rent in twain, fell upon the startled combatants. The floor had yielded to the immense pressure, and a yawning chasm presented itself to the horrified vision of the few, who, still in imminent peril, clung to the windows and broken beams. The platform, and that part of the house reserved for ladies, escaped the fearful crash, which had swept Rebels rampant, Rebels timorous, fearless Union men, and quasi Union men, into one common pit, where death in hideous guise held high carnival. The choking dust, which filled the air, the piercing shrieks of women, the heavy groans from the suffocating, struggling mass of humanity beneath the fallen floor, the pen refuses to detail.

Come with me, reader, to the scene of this dire calamity at the setting of the sun on this eventful day. The last of the mangled corpses, alas! so crushed, that not a human lineament can be traced, is being drawn from the debris; and a night of bitter gloom shrouds the city, which the dawn found teeming with exultant life.

Thus the programme for the 7th of July read: An execution was to come off, as the sun wheeled into the zenith; as the day cooled, a military pageant was to fill the streets with martial strains and war-loving people; and with night was anticipated the presentation of a flag to the pet regiment of the county. But the curtain fell upon muffled drums, stricken mourners, and open graves!

In happy contrast with the wretchedness which filled so many households, was the room where mother, *sons*, and little sister Winnie, clasped in each others' arms, gave God thanks for this signal manifestation of the protecting love he has promised to the widow and fatherless; they had sorely felt the sorrow, which endureth but a night; the joy, which cometh in the morning, was now theirs.

In an adjoining room lay one of the victims of the morning's catastrophe. With heroic endurance, Harry Blout suffered the mutilation of his hand to save life, and, with cheerful fortitude, bore the dissecting knife. Over his couch Maggie, with tender, womanly care, bends; and, conquering all repugnance to the sight of blood and quivering muscle, so inherent in a woman's nature, unshrinkingly holds the filling bowl, and dripping instruments.

Farther on, in a darkened chamber, lay another. The wound had been probed, the ball extracted, and now Richard Whedden, with closed eyes, reviews the scene of the morning and his miraculous escape.

In crying aloud the wrongs impious men were practising upon the masses, untutored, but jealously tenacious of their rights; in nerving the hearts of these plain, artless men to grasp Liberty's sword and battle for her truths, he had won for himself the sweet consciousness of having done his duty, and the inexpressible joy which Mercy leaves in the heart she has roused to overthrow cruelty.

Cato, when bending over the prostrate form of an idolized son, exclaimed, " What pity is it one can die but once for one's country!" Richard Whedden, stretched upon a couch of pain by a traitor's hand, thanked Heaven that he had been counted worthy to suffer for his country; and, God willing, with health and strength, he would rise a firm defender of truth and justice mid scenes—

> "Where stern Oppression lifts her iron hand,
> And restless cruelty usurps command."

CHAPTER IX.

THE SWAMPS A RETREAT FOR LOYALISTS.

WE will now go back to the city and trace events which followed the trial and its accompanying calamity. Francis Bierce was duly informed that the prisoner had either made good his escape, or, what was more probable, was among those so fearfully mutilated as not to be recognized, and now buried.

The next question was, who, and where were the men who dared draw in defence of "tyranny and Abe Lincoln?" A thorough search was instituted for the "traitors," but proved unsuccessful.

It was a stubborn fact, and one generally accredited, that scores of men in the surrounding country were daily leaving their customary pursuits, plantations, and homes, to conceal themselves in the mountains; and, report said, preparing to take the field *en masse*, when the time should come to aid the Yankee invader; therefore a picked guard was set to watch, with unslumbering vigilance, every avenue of approach to these fastnesses. Days went by, and, as no arrests were made, the watch grew daily less wary.

It was night, and the sheep on the hill-top, no longer caressed by the flickering, dancing light of the bivouac fire, looked down and saw Liberty swing wide the vast portal of her mountain ranges and lead on *braves* in paths, still echoing to the tread of those gone on before. Not a bivouac fire, not a challenge, not a sentinel! No sound, save the tramping of feet treason could not shackle, broke the stillness.

To cities and towns came the astounding news of the disappearance of the guard to a man!

Where were they! Go to the loyal sons of Carolina, now fighting for the nation's life, — *they* can tell. Double the price set on "traitors'" heads, — double the guard, — double the vigilance, but of no avail; for Liberty, with her shining cohorts, leads on the van! while treason's minions bivouac in vain on the outskirts of her retreat, nor dare pierce the shadow which she leaves behind.

* * * * * *

In the firm belief that the impending blow, which the "Grand Northern Army" was to wield at Manassas, would effectually wipe out the Rebellion, men, who from physical inability could not brave the mountaineer's life, tore themselves from loving arms, and sought the secure retreat which the cypress swamps afforded. From these almost impenetrable morasses prodigious trees loom up, whose limbs are covered with a grayish moss, several feet in length, and in such quantities as to curtain a safe abode for one or more runaways. In and around, the rattlesnake, and his no less venomous companions, the moccason, black-runner, and copper-head, keep guard, signalling intruding footsteps with the deadly rattle or terrifying hiss. In such secure haunts Black Dick and Yellow Dine meet, — both runaways from cruel masters or brutal overseers; each, perhaps, representatives of different counties, but each alike seeking refuge from the white man's tyranny. As with the entire race, with few exceptions, courtship and the marriage ceremony are abridged to the simple formula, "be my woman, Rose," "ask massa, Sam," so these poor souls meet, and, resigning all former ties, Dick takes unto himself a new wife. Driven from the haunts of man by man's unrestrained violence, nature takes the wanderers into her lap and lavishly spreads her mosses for a screen by day and a couch for night. Birds of rare plumage and rapturous note fill the dim woods with melody; while fruits and luscious berries hang temptingly near, and, falling at the touch, fill the hungry soul with nectarian juices. No mammoth task, no stinted rations, no lash, no bleeding back and groaning pallet, here await runaways, but liberty and life, free and joyous, over acres of soil the traveller fears and shuns with hurried feet; and the hunter with spurred heel urges on his jaded beast, lest dark night should find him wrapt in the spectral-haunted shadows, which steal up from these interminable wastes.

It was a fearful hour, for a tornado swept the land. Houses were unroofed, fences prostrated, and the tasseled corn, and blooming cotton-patch laid low. A sturdy oak, which had braved many a blow, mightier than this, in years past, yielded to the blast, and "crashing, thundering, shook the ground."

"God be praised!" rose simultaneously from many grateful hearts; for the threatened danger, just escaped, offered a temporary retreat for the pursued. The unfrequented road, down which they fled, was now rendered impassable by the fallen tree; for it was sheer madness for their pursuers to strike out into the forest which bordered the road on either side on such a wild, dark night.

A score of men, panting with the fierce excitement of the deadly chase, crept beneath the boughs of the prostrate oak, and, in mud mid leg-deep, laid down,— and it was time; for a lull in the tempest brought to their strained ears the tramp of approaching horsemen. Soon a body of men appeared, the lightning playing upon their weapons, — for they were heavily armed, — making their faces glare out horribly beneath their limp, water-soaked caps.

The barrier, which neither man nor beast could surmount, was met with a volley of oaths. "Halt!" was shouted, as others came dashing up; "the devils have escaped us! Back to the fork! — down to the left? We'll have them, yet!"

The savage threat which silenced one or two, who declared they had seen objects creeping down the road after passing the fork, left no room for farther suggestions or aught but implicit obedience. The hunters turned upon their steps and sought the left fork; they found it, doubtless, but not the mud-soaked, exultant creatures, who crawled from about the huge tree, and, with mighty strides and laughter-ringing shouts, defiant of storm and farther pursuit, pressed on for the "big swamp."

The East was kindling with roseate light, when our band of patriots, with hearts swelling with gladness for dangers past and mercies near, reached and plunged into the thickest part of the welcome morass. Sinking into the soft, spongy soil, springing upon some inviting log, to jump as quickly from it, as the king-snake, his domain being so rudely assailed, crawls out therefrom, and, with glistening eye and arching neck, strikes terror into the hearts of the intruders, — widely they scatter. Pitching, tumbling, floundering, tied up, thrown down by the thick hanging vines, these dauntless ones push on; for succor is nigh, and hope warms the heart and makes the ills of the hour the subject of jest and hearty good-humor.

To the hunter, to the naturalist, whom the fox or some rare species of bird tempts to their borders, these swamps seem impenetrable. "No human foot," say they, "can pierce such a wilderness; for if once entangled in the matted verdure, which often conceals dark pools, extrication is impossible, death sure." But dangers, such as the pleasure-seeker turns shudderingly from, make men, hunted and denounced, bold to encounter, and fearless to brave every ill, than to suffer a crucifixion of the soul.

Suddenly the leader stops and bends low. A long, sweet note escapes him, which is answered by the shrill piping of the quail: the well-known signal is followed by rousing cheers, and the hanging mosses of a cluster of trees, but a few rods from the wanderers, part, and disclose the retreat of the vociferous band, which leaps forth, — and fathers, sons, friends, neighbors, alike supporters of liberty and union, meet.

CHAPTER X.

PRESENTATION OF A FLAG.

NEVER did a more brilliant throng grace Gaston Hall than on this night, — the one which is to witness the presentation of the flag, and which unforeseen events had deferred. Flags, rich in satin fold and golden tassel, heavy with bars (but not luminous, for the greater part are starless), festoon the walls, and flowers of rich color and ravishing fragrance, the triumphal arches, which span the rostrum, where soft light, perfumes from innumerable wreaths, and secesh devices of costly jewels, bestow a charm, which nought save the presence of the belle of the season, the presenter of the flag and suite, could enhance.

Gaslight, that unsurpassed beautifier, shines down upon beauty and grace, richly attired in gossamer fabrics; on aristocratic general-officers, whose gray uniforms shine with the badges of their profession; on privates, glorying in the braided sleeve, where fair hands have wrought, with exquisite skill, the letters of the cause for which they have pledged their lives; and upon citizens, very happy and very boastful of coming victories. At a word of command, the crowd draws back, and, amid a wild burst of music, the graceful fluttering of handkerchiefs, and prolonged cheering, the gallant 7th moves down the hall and forms about the *estrade*. All eyes turn upon the distant curtain, which, rising from the lower arch, discloses a bright and beautiful vision.

Amid the cloud-like drapery, which, in soft undulations, wraps the willowy forms of the attending *ton*, stands the tall, dignified Helen Bierce, severely, plainly dressed in *homespun* —

> "With no bewitching curls, kissing as they go
> Her brow, her cheek, her bosom of snow."

With no clear drops appending to the ear, no bracelet, or precious pin, but clothed in a cotton frock — the work of her own hand — she, the cynosure of all eyes, meets the unaffected stare of the crowd, and, with irresistible appeal, calls the eye-worship of the throng to her face, which a truly earnest soul lights up with a beauty indescribable.

As the regimental flag is placed in her hand, and with inimitable grace she steps forward to present it, the motive, which prompted this self-sacrificing courage, bursts upon the crowd, and vociferous shouts and overwhelming clapping followed. "Col. Blassing," she said, "to you, the commander of this regiment, our hearts' love, to be our State's boast, we give this flag; we, who have made it, and consecrated it to Liberty, ask of you, its brave defenders, to place it upon the dome of the Capitol at Washington, where floats the flag of a once happy, united people, now a thing despoiled and hateful to our sight. It has been said, and truly, that the want of everything is fully made up by the spirit of the cause, and the soul within stands in place of discipline, organization, resource. Such is the spirit, which animates every breast in our young Confederacy. We may be crippled and impoverished by our powerful adversary; but *we cannot be conquered*, and scorn defeat! Our noble Beauregard calls you for the great struggle at Manassas; we bid you go to meet a foe relentless, vindictive, unscrupulous, to suffer, to die for your cause, and the honor of your mothers, your wives, your sisters. And shall we be unmindful of the price of blood and treasure which our liberty demands? No! the duty the God of battles enjoins upon us, shall be unflinchingly met; our jewels, our once valued gems, we throw into the common treasury, and, discarding the luxuries of which you are deprived, clad in the durable work of our own hands, await duty's call to the hospital, or amid burning shot and shell to carry the cup of cold water; and if need comes, with arms in our hands, to fight bravely by the side of fathers, husbands, brothers; for living we will be victorious, or dying, our deaths shall be glorious."

The gay and dashing Colonel received the colors and replied gallantly, handsomely referring to the noble example the presenter had that night set for the mothers and daughters of the South. In conclusion, he said: "This banner, dear to us all, shall by our blood be defended, and, God willing, not only over Washington, but over every foot of Northern and Southern soil shall the Bonny Blue Flag wave, proclaiming to the world the life, the unsullied honor, the mercy and sovereignty of our glorious Confederacy."

The main feature of the evening over, gay forms flitted down from high galleries, and with braves, "so handsome and manly to view," sweep the floor in the mazy round of the dance. Under festooned arches, in shadowy corners forgotten by the revellers, in the dimly lighted robing-room, low earnest words are breathed. The lingering pressure of the hand, the "blush of consent," which speaks in silent eloquence to the heart of the brave pleader, the rapturous embrace which the morrow's departure sanctions, the vows of eternal love, the wild pulse-beats of hearts, so soon to burn, to expire amid the fierce tumult of battle, why further depict?

CHAPTER XI.

A MISTAKE IN A PROFESSION.

BEHOLD us once more in Maggie Blout's parlor. She sits waiting Harry's return from the hall; he enters even now, and, chiding her for her grave looks, draws her to his side.

"And you will go with the regiment to-morrow?" Maggie asked, struggling to keep back the tears, which formed beneath the long silken lashes.

"I must."

"But you are incapacitated for the field," she said, gently pressing the maimed arm; "say that you will not go, dear Harry," she pleaded.

"Hear what I have to tell you, dearest, then you will cease to urge me to remain idle at home. Of the political state of America I knew little before coming here; and what has come to my knowledge since, without the seeking, was enough to convince me it was for my interest and peace of mind to shun lukewarm partisans as well as radicals. Never did I for a moment entertain even a vague surmise that the antagonism of the rival factions of North and South, though so fierce and bitter, would culminate in open rebellion; but the truth that it *would* do so was forced home to me some months since, when conceding to your uncle's request, although in direct opposition to my own feelings, I entered the Court-house to hear, as was announced for the evening, an eminent speaker on the one subject of the hour — 'The despotic influence of a majority.' What, he said, would be the despotism of the North, should the election of Abraham Lincoln be secured; and of the long-continued and increasing usurpations of those who made, and as unscrupulously broke, laws of their own caprice, tyrannizing at will over the South, because the weaker of the two, could be summed up in these few words,—*Do as I bid, if you would live!* The man before us, Maggie, was a powerful speaker, and the intensity of his zeal was such as to win disciples to any creed he might advance; and at his concluding words, 'Let the South band themselves together and the North will cease to be the masters; cold, calculating, mercenary, unmilitary as they are, they will find themselves powerless to coerce and resist us.' I felt it was the bounden duty of the South to go out from such an association, peaceably, if she could, forcibly, if she must. Under this fearful delusion I threw into the treasury what, now that my eyes are no longer blinded, made my hands *red* — red as the hands of those who, not blindly, there cast in with me; for ignorance is no excuse for my mad act."

Harry stopped, and for several moments walked the floor, fuming silently; then throwing himself again upon the settee by Maggie's side, he resumed : —

"The morning following the lecture, I met Richard Whedden, and rode with him to his house. Before we parted, the scales one by one fell from my eyes, and I knew I had been fearfully and wholly misled;

that not "right," but "rule or ruin," was the *shibboleth* on every lip of those whose cause I had espoused. Would to God, before I had lifted one finger to aid these robbers, these murderers, my life had been taken! Now my life, my all, is pledged to atone for that irreparable blunder."

"Harry, it was a deplorable mistake, still, much good has come of it; your giving so generously, has allayed all suspicion of your real sentiments, and enabled you to secure the retreat of scores of persecuted men from the State; beside preserving my house from the intrusion of military detectives."

"That much I have done, Maggie, and I go out to-morrow, secure in the confidence of the Rebels, to strike when and where the most effective blow may fall."

"Strike *for* those you stand arrayed against? that will indeed be hazardous."

"Yes, with all the power Liberty lends to man for her defence."

"But, found in the active volunteer service of North Carolina, you will suffer."

"No matter what I may suffer, I have the spirit to brave all fate may have in store for me. Say, have you forgotten the wild life I led when a boy?"

"I know your courage and intrepidity, but—"

"But what? Say on."

"You may be shot, and in some hospital languish uncared for. See here," she added, rising and drawing a serge garment from beneath the settee, "you say duty calls you to the field; as imperative a one makes me join the corps of nurses, which leaves here to-morrow for Manassas."

"Maggie!"

"Nay, Harry, I have besought you to stay at home where your own interest and others' require your presence, but you must go, you say; so must I. Do not look so grave, nor make an attempt to dissuade me, — my determination cannot be changed."

"Have you counted the cost of such self-sacrifice?" Harry said, to break the painful pause which followed Maggie's avowal.

"Yes, thrice over. The agony of suspense is intolerable; the labor of nursing the sick, comforting: it is for you, and you alone, that I go into camp or hospital — anywhere to serve you best."

"Your affection for me, Maggie, priceless as it is, must not induce you to neglect higher duties at home; next to you, in my heart's love, comes Richard Whedden. To serve me best is to watch over him, to conceal him from the villains on his track."

"And leave you to the neglect of hirelings, if sick or wounded?"

"Neither, Maggie; I shall come back to thank you, under God's mercy, for my friend's life."

After a short, but painful struggle, the promise "to stay" was given; and, to interrupt the expressions of gratified affection which followed, Maggie said: "Enough of ourselves, dear Harry. Now tell me of your two special charges, Charles Coxe and Mr. Whedden."

"Charles Coxe, thank Heaven, has made good his escape. I saw the negro, who acted as guide to Coxe and his men, to-day. Though hotly pursued, he said they eluded the armed gang on their track, and reached the swamp in safety."

"This is indeed good news; and now of Mr. Whedden. Is not the search for him given over yet?"

"No: and I fear never will be. He is safe here for the present only."

"Has his property been confiscated?"

"Yes: I bought what he valued most, and left it in the house."

"His horse, what became of that?"

"I take him with me to-morrow."

"Then all of Blout's Rifles can turn cavalry if they choose?" said Maggie, archly.

"No indeed. I do about as I please. The horses which you saw on the morning of the hunt were hired for the occasion; if I mistake not, these men will see the time when they'll wish for horses, or winged feet. The North know our strength, and go doubly armed to meet us; the fighting will be no boy's play, Maggie; for on the issue of this coming battle, I confidently believe, hangs a nation's life or death. Now to business," he added; "see how late the night."

At this moment a servant entered, and handed her mistress a note. She took it, and at Harry's request, as it was from Helen Bierce, read it aloud:—

"The torture of the evening is over, the arrangements for the morrow complete, and I am weary and sick at heart. O Maggie, shall I ever be reconciled to dear, dear Willie's death? Had he fallen at his post, my wicked, rebellious heart would check its grief; but to be crushed, to be suffocated is awful! I cannot stay here longer. I have sold my nag, my jewels, my wardrobe — all I own — and leave in the early train for Richmond. My life, so wretched, shall be spent at the pallet of our sick soldiers. Come to me, dear cousin; I am so sad to-night — the last in my father's house. Discarded from his love, the idol of my heart buried, with no one to kiss me good-by, I go wretched, unloved, alone! I heard your cousin say, as he passed me on the hall steps: "he left with his regiment." These are his last hours with you; therefore do not hesitate to refuse my request, if in my selfishness I ask too much. If you do not come, write me one loving word. To be forgotten by all but you is my earnest wish. HELEN."

The silence which followed the reading of the note, was broken by Harry's saying: "For once in my life I must acknowledge, I have misjudged a woman. The petted, spoilt child of fortune passed out of sight, when Helen Bierce, in defiance of her father's threat, said "No," on that memorable morning. It cost her the affection of a fearfully depraved parent,— but for that one act of heroism she will feel fully repaid, when awakened to a sincere conviction of her duty." Then rising, he rang for the carriage, adding, "I can spare you for a few hours, for Miss Helen needs you. Just five minutes for bonnet and shawl, not a moment over," Maggie heard, as the door closed after her.

CHAPTER XII.

FAMILY HISTORY.

The world said, Mrs. Tull loved her riches with the fervor of adoration. Born heir to thousands of acres, and as many negroes to till them; taught from infancy, that to lack money was to lack a passport into the pleasant places of God's earth; taught also to look upon poverty as a crime, a scar, and its subject the despicable mark of the world's scorn and reprobation, she consequently had no use for any, save the well-to-do in the world, and would shun the plea of the suffering poor, as she would the viper's sting. She had married to increase her wealth; and, when death took from her side the one she had vowed to love, — ay, love for his gold, — no grief or bitter reflection pierced her unnatural heart.

The "diamond widow" needed no long wooing; the richest of her suitors bore away the prize amid the hearty congratulations of friends, — and Helen Bierce had a new mother.

Within a year, Helen and her two brothers were sent North to school. Annually their father visited them; his wife never.

Years passed. On a return trip from New York, the proud father led his beautiful daughter to her mother's side, thinking, witless man, the admiration she everywhere elicited, would at least command respect from his heartless wife. But her charms so completely eclipsed the mother's, that no other emotion but intense jealousy was aroused, and she took no pains to conceal it.

Helen had no love for the selfish being, who had made herself and her brothers aliens from home; and, but for her father's urgent entreaty, would have never gone back to a roof, once hallowed by a fond mother's love, now overshadowed by the sin of a corrupt woman.

Judicious training and education had much modified Helen's imperious disposition; but the air of the North could not cool her blood; and it was with many secret misgivings Mrs. Winn — the truly Christian lady to whose care she had been entrusted — saw her young and gifted charge removed from the quiet seclusion of her own home, and gentle but firm restraint, to mingle with the world.

Helen's return to her father's house was soon followed by that of her brothers. Ralph, the elder, was a cold, stern man. Had he been blessed with the, gentle care and cherishing love of the mother who bore him, instead of being left to the neglect of a mercenary Northern teacher, he would doubtless have been other than we have to portray him.

How Helen's heart ached, when, the first fond greeting over, she saw the change years had wrought in her bold but generous-hearted brother. She had felt he was changed, for of late years his letters had grown strangely cold and short. She should see him, she thought, then all would be explained. But when they met, her pleading eyes, her tremulous voice, were passed by unnoticed; no assuring smile to banish forebodings, no loving word came, only the chilling look, which silenced every inquiry his haughty reserve excited.

To Willie, Helen turned, and in that fond heart found the ever-ready sympathy, the loving response her kindly nature craved. Like his sister, William Bierce had found kind friends in his Northern home, and now he had returned to his native State, to gladden at least one heart there, — his sister Helen's.

Very proud was the father of his boy, who had left the North, rejoicing in the high honors his cadetship at West Point had won; but his mother passed him by as she did his sister, "having no use for such."

"What has the North done to provoke the South to secede, do you ask, boy?" said Mr. Bierce to his son, who, to stop the storm of abuse, which was daily heaped upon him for not volunteering, had ventured the question. "What has the North done?" he repeated; "look to her progressive usurpations, so long, so uncomplainingly borne by us. What are they? Why, enormous tariffs, unconstitutional, oppressive, unjust, which fill Northern vaults with golden ingots, but beggar the South; the fishing bounty, which we pay, and New England Yankees reap; the navigation laws, which carry all trade to Northern marts, compelling us to go up thither to be swindled and jewed by the insane cupidity of a community, which has no higher aspiration than commercial gain; and, more than all this, a people, who trample under foot the law, which requires the return from the Free States of fugitive slaves to their masters; send into our midst abolitionists, 'demons reared in the blackest smoke of hell,' to incite our slaves to rise and murder us, our wives, and little ones, with the promise of our lands, if the butchery is thorough and clean! This is what the North is doing now, and has been doing for years, and what we say shall no longer be done! We have lifted our voice, but of no avail, — we now lift our hands, — let the North beware!"

"And it is such as *you*, Francis Bierce," cried the young man, springing to his feet, as the door closed after the elder Bierce, his face flushed with the righteous anger, which fired his words, — "that have swept the South through, kindling the incendiary fires of rebellion by such mischievous misrepresentations and falsehoods! It is such as *you*, who, with shotted weapons, dodged Abe Lincoln's steps from his native State to the Capitol at Washington, while your minions stood at their guns, waiting the electric word to peal out, to thunder through the land, *the monster — dead!* Ay, and it is such as you, who, with bloody hearts but cleanly hands, left Washington the night of March the 4th — *defeated!* but loud in your boasts that, when next you entered *there*, every building, then teeming with Northern vandals, should be razed to the ground!"

Foolish, foolish William Bierce! stay thy tongue, or such ebullitions of indignant feeling will cost thee thy young life. Don the gray livery, as hundreds of others have done to save themselves from abuse; so the heart is bold and strong in the right, it cannot contaminate. Snap thine eyes wrathfully at the braided sleeve, where with exquisite skill is wrought C. S. A., which thou hast promised to wear; those who *know* thee, know the wearing of it is no concession to the mandate of the arch-traitor Davis, but to the persistent entreaty of a sister, whose idol thou art; so be reconciled to the traitor's garb, for with such armor thou canst best serve thy cause, relieve the suffering, and defeat many a well-laid scheme of those thou dost fraternize with.

A month later sees our prediction verified.

Mr. Bierce had fitted out a privateer, and desired his son to command her. This he resolutely refused to do; but, at the unceasing solicitation of his sister, he finally gave his consent to go as mate.

The "Pigeon" sailed mid the booming of cannon and shouts from the shore. Long after the crowd had dispersed, Helen Bierce walked the landing; she loved the sound of the waves, which had borne her Willie from her; softly lapping the wharf, where she stood, they seemed to bear away with them to the mighty deep, one a tear, another a sorrow, until the weight which crushed her heart was gone. With a last fond look turned upon the vanishing sails of the privateer, these words escaped her: —

"Do your duty fearlessly, Willie; I have done mine in urging you to this step, — and God bless us both."

The "Pigeon" had been but four days out, when the intrepid mate made the attempt to scuttle her. "Better that all should perish," he said, "than lend themselves to piratical sins."

The attempt proved abortive. One night an alarm of fire rung through the ship; but, by the unwearied exertions of desperate men, she was saved. A day later the pilot was missing, and the "Pigeon" struck firm and fast on the bar; but again the Evil One lent a helping hand and set her afloat. So much ill-luck did attend the fated ship, the desponding crew were about to set sail for home for repairs, when the cheering cry of "Sail ho!" from the look-out, roused the crew's failing courage and fiendish instincts.

With all sail set, the "Pigeon" bore down on the unarmed craft and silenced all opposition to entering a Southern port, by the show of formidable guns. Another white-winged victim fell into the power of that piratical crew, and the "Pigeon" set sail home with her valuable prizes.

Since the disappearance of the pilot, so vigilant was the watch set, that young Bierce was compelled to abandon further attempts to bring summary vengeance upon the buccaneers.

We next meet this brave, loyal soul in secesh livery, urging home a besotted companion; and still again in the crowded Court-house, mistake those who were near, heard amid the fierce tumult of that morning, his shout, — "The Union and Abe Lincoln forever!" as he went down amid the struggling, fighting mass, which sunk beneath the broken floor.

When his manly form was drawn from the ruins, suffocation had done its work, — a black and stiffened corpse he lay!

CHAPTER XIII.

MOTHER AND DAUGHTER — MISTRESS AND SLAVE.

In her boudoir, Mrs. Bierce, just returned from the gay scene at Gaston Hall, reclines. The richness of her attire, however, lends no charm to her haughty, disturbed face.

Vine, a spruce-looking quadroon chamber-maid, answers her violent summons.

"Please, Missis, Miss Helen is busy, and can't come."

"Go back, Vine, you nigger! and tell her I say, Come directly."

Mrs. Bierce, always impatient of delay, was to-night more irritable than usual; and, as Vine still delayed, she sprung to the bell-rope, exclaiming: "Hateful niggers, I wish the North had every one of you! and you, Vine, I heard you whisper to Jane the other night, 'it wasn't for long you'd have such a cross old missis.' I'll see if you will use my name again in that way: these Yankee notions I shall take upon myself to whip out of you." Then looking at her watch, "you shall have your first lesson to-night, for Francis will not be at home for two hours yet;" and again she attacked the bell.

So fierce was the jerk, the heavy tasselled cord flew

from its fastening, and struck with no gentle force upon the head of the excited lady, driving a pin, which held her massive braids, deep into her flesh. The pain and the sight of blood, which trickled down her white neck, roused all the passions of her turbulent nature, and at the sound of approaching footsteps, she sprung to the door, exclaiming, "You shall smart for this, Vine!"

After the duties of the day were over, Vine's custom was to steal down to the servants' quarters and relieve herself of the day's budget of news.

Once she had been hired out, and during that time had secretly been taught to read. As she possessed a remarkably retentive memory, she was eagerly sought after by the servants in the Square, who congregated at nights in some spacious kitchen or unoccupied hut, and in smothered tones talked of the Yankees coming to set them free, and of the Northern homes made ready for them. This night the sable group is larger than usual; and, as Vine still lingers in the big house, and the thought is forced home that she may not come at all, their dark faces grew frightfully ugly, as seen in the flickering light of the pine knot on the hearth. From the look-out, near the barred door, the girl is discerned at length tripping down the steps; now lost in the shade of the elms, to emerge into the broad moonlight, which silvers the brick walk her swift feet scarcely touch. The door cautiously opens, and, with low exclamations of delight, their oracle seats herself in their midst.

"There," she cries, "do hear Missis' bell! here, you, Zip, you go hold the clapper till I'se through, and here's a sixpence for you." Then turning to the group — "Missis did n't mind the news much to-day, she's so full of her own self; but while I'se dressin' her hair, I used my eyes handy. The Yankees is comin', every one of them, to kill every man that's got niggers; the North is fighting for the niggers and nobody else; they swear they can whip the South all to nothin', and we shall be free and fine as white folks. There! I read them very words, and every one is as solemn and true as these big bumps. See here (stripping up her sleeve), this is what I gets for what Missis calls laziness. When I reads the good news, I forgets my fingers, but not long; it takes Missis to scatter a pretty dream." A sympathetic groan from the dusky audience has the desired effect, and Vine is to-night more garrulous than ever; and, after telling all she knew, and a great deal which was only conjecture, she finished, saying: "And Miss Helen won't stay here no longer. I saw Kizzie packing her trunk, and she told me she was going away with young missis, and neither of them was coming back no more. Poor Miss Helen! Massa William's death has wellnigh killed her; old massa ought to be hanged for looking so cross at her as he does, because she would n't swear to somethin' about that abolition man. Hark! if there is n't his call now for Jim, and I must cut for missis' room. Golly! what a tearing rage she's in! but who cares for Missis when Massa's here."

With a merry laugh Vine left the group, and, spinning the promised sixpence at the head of Zip, who, perched upon a chair in the long hall, was with his might doing her bidding, she bounded up the broad flight of stairs, which led to her mistress' room, with the fleetness of a gazelle.

To return to Mrs. Bierce, whom we left in no enviable state of mind, awaiting her maid's reappearance. She was near the door when it opened, and her daughter entered. "So you've come at last!" she screamed, as she seized Helen, in her blind fury, mistaking her for Vine, who was but a shade darker, and quite as fresh looking; "I'll skin you alive! I will! and we'll see if your master dares—"

"Unhand me, woman! Are you mad, that you take me for Vine?"

Helen's voice calmed the enraged being before her; she quickly dropped her arm, and staggered to a chair.

"I thought you were Vine, Helen," she said at length. "You know you do resemble a nigger; oh my poor head (by way of covering her face to escape the withering look which was cast upon her) "why don't you hand me something to ease it?"

Helen did not move; very white and calm she stood, tapping the floor with her slippered foot. Presently she said:—

"I came here at your bidding; what is your wish?"

"I sent for you some half hour since, that I might be the bearer of the good tidings, that your father has signified his consent to overlook the past, and take to his heart his Helen, so becomingly dressed in the work of her own hands;"—then scanning her closely—"all the colors of the rainbow, well stirred up in cotton web, is truly appropriate mourning for your dear Willie; but no matter, so long as the scantiness of material finely displays the contour of so voluptuous a form!" and a light, mocking laugh followed the taunting words. But words and laughter fell alike unheeded upon the silent girl. Thoroughly provoked by Helen's passive indifference, her merciless tormentor then hurled her bitter venom at the only vulnerable spot so sinful a tongue could reach, — her affection for her deceased brother.

"Hold, woman!" she cried, tortured beyond all endurance. "Speak not that sacred name here. I have borne insults from you long and patiently for my father's sake, but that is over now; this is the last night we spend beneath the same roof. I go, and you have the joy, if so depraved a heart can experience such an emotion, of seeing the complete consummation of all your projects; I go from my father's roof, fully resolved never to enter his house again, while you are its mistress."

Not caring to witness the triumphant smile, which she knew her words would awaken, Helen turned from the room. As she left the door, Vine entered by another into her mistress' presence, and, before Helen could reach her own room, a sound, which could not be mistaken, followed by a heavy fall, made her turn quickly upon her steps, and re-enter the boudoir.

At the same moment a carriage drove up to the house, and a gentleman and lady alighted.

"Helen, dear Helen, look up! Am I not welcome?"

The sweet, soft voice of Maggie Blout aroused the suffering girl; she raised her colorless face, exclaiming: "Maggie, is it you? Thank God, I have some one near to ease my breaking heart."

The approach of morn had awakened Night's drowsy sentinels, and, with a will, they were cheerily lifting the curtains of the eastern chamber, when

Maggie and her cousin rode away from Mr. Bierce's dwelling.

During their drive home, Harry Blout heard from Maggie the fearful scene which, a few hours before, had been enacted in the house they had just left.

"Was the girl much injured?" he asked.

"Yes; but Dr. Hall thinks, with proper care, she may eventually recover; she is to be removed to the hospital to-day. Helen has been prevailed upon to remain at home; consequently, uncle Francis and his wife leave immediately for the country; and, as Vine not infrequently attends them on their journeys, her absence will not be remarked. When they return, some kind of a story will be gotten up, — either that she was too saucy to keep and was sold, or she sickened and died, and so the matter will drop. O Harry, what greater evil could be visited upon man than slavery? It is truly a foe to religion, a despoiler of morality, and, as we have proof, almost daily, makes the master, be he man, woman, or child, a despot of the highest grade. God grant, if this war must be, that it may ultimately and completely do away with slavery."

A few hours later and Harry was gone; but Maggie still lingered at the window, from which she had leaned, to wave a last adieu as the cars swept by.

"I shall come back, Maggie," lingered upon the lips of the one, whose dark eye moistened as he returned the loving salute; and Maggie *felt* his last words were prophetic.

CHAPTER XIV.

ESCAPE OF MRS. WEASEL — FINDS A FRIEND.

On the following morning, Maggie was awakened before light by her servant. "Dare was a woman down stairs," she said, "dat wants to see missis."

"Who can she be?" exclaimed the startled girl.

"She did n't give no name, missis; but she 'pears awful anxious like."

"Did she come alone?"

"No, missis; she has a boy wid her. See, har's a slip o' paper for you."

Maggie glanced at the few words, then said, hurriedly, "Tell the good lady to come here directly, — but stay; who admitted these strangers?"

"Me let 'em in; no other soul don't know they's har."

"I am so glad, aunty, and do not speak of this to anyone."

"Neber you fear, Missis; old Liz is as black as the grave and as hush, too; she neber tells nobody's secrets and she'd die all ober 'fore she'd tell yer's."

"I know it, aunty; and now that the time has come for great caution, your wise eyes and open ears must be my hedge. Go now and bring the lady and boy here; there is work for us both, and we must be about it."

Nothing pleased the old servant so well, as to be told she was of much account to her mistress; and the thought that she looked to her to fill master Harry's place, sent the rheumatic old body spinning down the broad stair-case as if youthful vigor and not infirm old age turned the key of locomotion.

Lizzie, or aunt Lizzie, as Maggie loved to call her, was ripe in years and good works; she had been a faithful nurse to Maggie's mother, and at her dying bedside had received into her arms her infant daughter. "Promise me, Lizzie," said the sinking mother, "that you will be to my babe what you have ever been to me, and I die happy;" the mother heard the promise given, and on the devoted servant and her charge, her last, fond gaze rested.

A mother's love and servant's fidelity were repaid by the strong affection Maggie ever manifested for her black nurse; and when, after her father's death, —she told Lizzie she was to be free, with money enough to live comfortably on, the remainder of her days, the old nurse fell on her knees and begged her young mistress to let her serve her always; she was rich enough, happy enough, she said, in dear missis's house, where she had promised dead missis to live for her babe and die for it, if the Lord willed.

Maggie, finding all remonstrance vain, finally told her she should never leave her; and that she might take the money she had reserved for her, and buy her husband if she could; and so old Jake was free. He hired himself out in the city, spending his Sundays with his wife and filling his heart with the praises of young Missis, which Lizzie's tongue never tired to utter.

"Should violent hands be laid on you or yours,

Maggie," said Harry, on leaving, " you need no more doughty champion than Aunt Lizzie."

"And Jake?" said Maggie, "is as honest as Lizzie, for all I know; he certainly possesses a fair share of her sagacity, and the fact of your having purchased his freedom, secures you a powerful ally in him; and be sure nothing in which you are concerned can transpire in the city, without his being conversant with and publishing it here."

But to return to Lizzie. Not long, and with the lady and her child, she reëntered her mistress' room. Maggie's charming ease of manner, and the kind sympathy her words and looks evinced, soon drew from the stranger the cause of her flight, and the imminent danger, which threatened her, should her steps be traced. Calmly Mrs. Weasel spoke of the atrocities practised upon herself and family, because her husband refused to volunteer, as well as all demands to equip troops. "When he was arrested," she said, "because of his Union principles, and thrown into jail, I could not murmur, for I felt he was safer in prison than out of it. With my children, I sought shelter in au untenanted house of my husband's; but my persecutors found me there, and made my life wretched with abuse; I should utterly have failed in courage, had it not been for a kind stranger, who heard of my distress and visited me. Through him I heard of my husband's well-being, and of the successful flight of my brother, Dr. Brown, with his family from the State. I speak of this noble young man to you freely, for I know he is your cousin."

"Neither are you unknown to me," said Maggie; "I have heard Harry speak of you often; and now, that he is no longer here to assist you, you must let me be your friend and protector."

"He told me to come to you in my extremity," — for the first time her voice trembled, — "I little thought it would be so soon."

"Don't cry, mamma," said the boy, who, with his head on his mother's knee, had been intently listening to what she had related; "I will tell the lady all the rest, it makes you cry so."

Maggie drew the little fellow to her side, and, smoothing his bright curls, said: "Yes, you shall tell me what has happened; then I shall know how best to aid you."

With childish eagerness, but with his eyes fixed upon his mother's bowed face, he said: "Mamma told Cora, that's little sis, and me, that when Mr. Blout's regiment went away, we should come to town to see him off; Mr. Blout was good to us, good almost as papa, and a great deal richer, I know."

"How do you know that?" Maggie asked.

"He gave mamma a heap of money, and when she would n't take it, he gave it to sis and me; it was a whole hundred; papa never gave us more than dollars, sometimes only shillings. Well, sis and me were up before mamma waked, and were in the city by sunrise; we promised, faithfully, we would keep out of the streets and stay hid, just where I knew the cars went through. I knew all about the cars, for I went with papa to Raleigh once. We had been hid a long time when we heard some music; then we knew the cars were coming. We were covered up by some alder-bushes, but we saw Mr. Blout lean from the car window and wave something white; Cora jumped up and threw the flowers we had picked, at him; he saw us, laughed, and kissed his hand, then the train was gone.

"Sis cried a little, but I told her papa said it was n't brave to cry, and she hushed; we picked honeysuckles awhile, then we got tired and fell asleep. Sis' crying woke me up, but I found I could not move, my hands and feet were tied with vines. A heap of boys were teasing Cora, pulling her hair, pinching her and tearing her frock; they were dreadful mean boys. I went to school where they did once, and they called me such bad names, and beat me so, papa took me away, and said I should go to school no more, until these bad times were over. Papa says, I am a strong boy for one of my age; I know I was pretty strong that time, for I snapped the vines almost as large as my thumb, and got at my knife, and cut them from my feet. I had my pistol in my pocket,—papa gave it to me, and taught me how to shoot too,—and I ran up to Jack White, and told him I'd shoot him if he kicked sis again. He said "he'd kicked her three times, and should kick the Yankee brat 'till she was dead." Just as he raised his foot I put up my pistol and shut my eyes; after the noise, I looked, and Jack lay on the ground very still."

"Oh, my son," groaned the weeping mother, "God would have punished him."

"He did, mamma; when I shut my eyes, I asked him to aim for me, and the shot went right into Jack; the boys all run away then, and I went up to Jack; I was glad he did n't move, for I had no more shot for him if he should hurt Cora again. She was bleeding awful, and, when I attempted to move her, she shivered all over. I saw a man coming up the road in a buggy; I stopped him, and asked him to take Sis home, she was so sick. He got down and went into the woods a little way; Cora had stopped groaning then, and never did anything, when he put his hand on her, and afterward bound up her head with his handkerchief. When he saw Jack White, he stepped up to where he lay; he said, he thought the boy was dead, and asked me 'who shot him?' I told him, 'he kicked Cora until she fell down, and said he would kill her; then I shot him.' 'Served him right, the scamp,' he said, and called me a brave boy; then he asked me whose children we were, and, when I told him, he turned quickly to his horse saying, 'Go home, and tell your mother all; Cora is badly hurt, but I will take good care of her, and drive round after night, and tell her how she is.' I ran with all my might, but had n't got through telling mamma, when we saw some men coming down the road horseback; mamma said, they were coming to the house. We fastened the doors and windows, and she took papa's revolver, and I my pistol, and we waited for them; they soon came up. I saw Jack White's father; he jumped down first, and came to the door; they all tried the door, and swore awful, because mamma would not open for them. She told them, they must tell her what they came for. They talked about me, and said they had come to get us both. Mamma said, she should fire upon the first one who broke into the house. But they did n't seem one bit afraid; I reckon they did n't know what a revolver she had. One man broke through the door, just where we were. He had got all in but one leg, when mamma fired, but it did n't hit him. I heard some one groan, though, outside of the door, where the ball went through. The big man was in then, and came right up to the table, on which mamma told me to stand. He had one hand on her shoulder, and the other, which held his revolver, was raised. I struck at it with my pistol, and the revolver fell to the floor. As the man reached down for it, mamma put out her foot; it went off, and the man rolled over on to the floor. Then we kept very still, to see what the men on the outside would do next. As we could hear nothing, we crept to the door, and I heard them call mamma a devil, and say the house was full of them, and they must set a guard about it, and send off to the city for more men. They shouted for Bill White, but he did n't answer, then one of them rode away. Two only were left, one was on the verandah and the other in the garden behind the house. Mamma whispered to me to load my pistol; that she was going to get out of the house and hide in the woods until night; but first, she said, she must frighten the guard away. She went up to the man on the floor and took the revolver out of his hand, and another bigger than that out of his belt. She fired right smart, and the man in the garden ran as she said he would, and we escaped from the house; crawled through the ditch in the garden and reached the woods unseen. While we were hid, I fell asleep; and when I opened my eyes it was night. Mamma said we must run for our lives, and we did. We would get tired and sit down, then run again. Just as it began to grow light we came out where the man had found Cora; and, in a little while, we came to your big house. Mr. Blout told us, if we came here, not to go into the city, any; and we came just as he said."

"And this is all?" said Maggie with a deep sigh, pressing the little fellow to her side.

A large tear on the boy's hand, made him look up, and the sympathy he read in those eyes, turned so lovingly upon him, made him bold to say, "Please ma'am, may the black woman give me something to eat? I had no dinner, nor no supper, all yesterday."

Lizzie entered, at this moment, with the morning's meal, which she spread temptingly before the wanderers. Only after the most urgent entreaty, was Mrs. Weasel prevailed upon to break her long fast; while Percy, overcame with excitement and fatigue, fell asleep with his food untasted; one hand holding the sweet cake his hungry stomach craved, but which the weary mouth refused to admit.

There Maggie and her guest sat long after the sun was up, the one comforting, the other growing strong with the bold confidence her hostess expressed, relative to her own and her children's safety in her house.

The mother's heart throbbed once more with hope, when she learned there were many in the city, as true to the Union as her husband and herself. "The influence of wealth and position now," said Maggie, "Secures them from sufferings, such as you have experienced, but let success crown another raid of the Rebels and all, who refuse to take up arms in defence of Southern rights, will be condemned as traitors, and treated as such. But, dear Mrs. Weasel, have no solicitude for your safety, so long as I have a house and the power to protect you; if the time should come, which sees me deprived of them here, we will seek protection and a home elsewhere;

and, rest assured, your little girl has fallen into kind hands; I have trusty servants, whom shortly I' will despatch for information of her."

Looking from the window as she spoke, she added joyfully, "here comes our old family physician! a better friend and counseller you could not have; I must speak to him in your behalf directly." And she left the room.

CHAPTER XV.

DR. HALL AND HIS PATIENT.

Dr. Hall was a man whom every one knew and honored, but no one feared. Secesh, respected him for his wealth and unbounded influence, and he duped them; Union men, denounced, penniless wanderers, sought him and were fed from his table, supplied with his gold, and by his keen sagacity helped out of the State; while forsaken wives and fatherless children blessed the good Samaritan, who, all unknown, kept the heart warm with shining messengers, which fed, housed, and clothed them.

On issuing from the sick-room he met Maggie. "I've seen your patient," he said, "and find you've minded me to the letter; he's twenty per cent better than his case promised yesterday;" then bending down to her ear he whispered, "its well he's mending; I'm mistaken, or another dawn finds him out of these snug quarters; I tell you they are again on his track, fiercer than ever! one of the d—— rascals told me, this morning, the Yankee Whedden wasn't in town, and this day's work was to scour the suburbs! that's what brought me here; say, now, are you ready for them?"

"Does Mr. Whedden know of his situation?" asked Maggie, with quickened breath.

"Yes, I found him strong enough for the whole dose; he swallowed it like a martyr; come! come! no more time talking; get up your fixings for a tramp."

"I must speak with you, doctor," persisted Maggie.

"Can't hear, can't hear, time is too precious to listen to a woman's rattle," and putting his hands to his ears, Dr. Hall began to ascend the stairs leading to the attic.

"But you *must* hear, doctor," and the resolute girl laid a firm, detaining hand upon his shoulder.

Dr. Hall turned, and reading the determination in her face, gave a low whistle; then patting her flushed cheek, said: "Blaze away! Maggie, I pity your sweetheart when you get up such a look as this."

"Have you heard of a Mr. White's being shot?" Maggie asked, in a sharp, quick voice.

"Bless your heart, girl! don't let that trouble you; that's an old story: it happened at least twelve hours ago, and not worth a fig compared to the work which we have on hand."

"Will you tell me the particulars?"

"Hang me, if I don't think you are demented! Ain't my hands full and my neck bare for a swing, if any of my irons should burn?"

But Maggie was decided; so, after grumbling a moment about woman's stick-to-a-tiveness, he resumed —

"Jack White — not a worse boy in town — was shot yesterday in the woods beyond here, by a boy, for beating his sister. Bill White, the boy's father, and a posse of men went to this boy's house — mind you, his father, Mr. Weasel, was shot last week at Salisbury, for trying to break jail; — he was a brave man! I knew him, — oh! I'm sorry, sorry for his family! Well, as I was saying, they beset the house, but the woman was ready for them. She was shrewd enough to get assistance before she was attacked. I saw one of the party after the affair; he said the shot fell thick as hail; one thing is certain, the men were driven off; and while waiting for reinforcements from the city to renew the attack, they lost their game; for the posse in the house made good their escape. When the house was broken open, White was found mortally wounded, and one of his accomplices not much better off in a room adjoining the one where White lay. They fired the house, and then set up such a hue and cry for this same woman and her allies, that if the Almighty has n't taken them under His mantle, they'll be caught, sure, and —"

"What? doctor."

"Murdered, of course; I declare for it," he said, musingly, "she was a brave one; I could fight for such a woman with a will."

"What would you do if she sought your protection?"

"Do! by St. Paul, I wish she had! What would I do? why arm her to the teeth, and bid her kill the monsters, who have slain her husband and burned her house to the ground! There, there, Miss curiosity, I've told my story, and see what a heat you've got me into; can't afford to let my energy work off in this way, when I've such a job on my hands, as this Whedden; but let me get him in a place of safety, and if that Mrs. Weasel escapes the dogs to-day, I'll find and help her out of the State, — let me alone for that!"

"But this same woman demands your aid now, doctor; to-morrow it will be too late."

"Who? what? this same woman! where is she! not in this house?" exclaimed the excited man, grasping Maggie by the arm.

"Yes, she is in this house; she wandered all night in the woods with her boy, and reached here before sunrise."

Dr. Hall dropped the arm, which he had grasped, and with his thumbs in the arm-sizes of his waistcoat, gave expression to his dumb-foundedness in "shucks" vociferously uttered. Recovering from his surprise, and rubbing his hands, he cried —

"Glad of it! glad of it! I'll father that woman and her young ones; just the right kind of material to spill one's blood for! — a life for a life. I'm in for that now!"

"Shall we come to that to-day? doctor."

"Chicken-hearted already!" he said, drawing Maggie down to his side, "Mrs. Weasel must put some of her fire into you."

"She has been under fire, remember that, doctor; give me a fair trial before you attach cowardice to me."

"So I will, so I will; but we shan't fight to-day, though we are coming to it, fast."

On the stairs the two sat, and in low earnest tones, laid their plans to outwit the murderers on the track of the afflicted ones, who demanded their counsel and protection, and whose safety as nearly concerned them as their own. What those plans were, they were successfully carried out, we must believe, or Maggie could not have entered her parlor, filled with armed men, as calmly as she did, a few hours after her consultation with Dr. Hall. The leader of the band of detectives, who thus assailed her house, was Ralph Bierce. His cold, searching gaze was returned with haughty surprise by Maggie, who, declining the proffered chair, said —

"Cousin Ralph, is it thus you enter my house, after so many long years of absence?"

"Duty, Margaret, is peremptory, not discretionary; in times like these, when traitors lurk in every house, the courtesies of life must be waived, the utmost rigor instituted to bring offenders under the law."

"And do you, and your armed friends, look to a defenceless woman's house as a rendezvous for such?" asked Maggie.

"It was reported, that Richard Whedden was among the number crushed to death the morning of the trial; but information has been received, that he still lives; to seek him, we are here, as it is quite natural to suppose that he has friends in neighbors so contiguous to his former residence."

"You have the right to draw such conclusions as you please," Maggie replied, coldly, "but those who knew aught of Mr. Whedden, knew that he led the life of a recluse."

"You have more knowledge of him, I see, than we," Ralph said, looking fixedly at her, "and we now propose to pursue our search here."

"Ralph, if my father were living, I should not be subjected to such an insult; his good name should spare his daughter the indignity of being treated as an abettor of sin in any guise."

"It is not to offer personal affront, but to satisfy the people, that we search here."

"I understand, perfectly, the popular voice sanctions the outrage of even our most sacred rights. Unprotected women, like myself, have no power to resist an armed force; but I do insist, that what you do here you do quickly; my servant will take the keys and open the house for your inspection, with the exception of my own chamber,—that, no strange foot shall enter."

The dignified, determined manner of the lady of the house checked any expression of opposition, which her words might have aroused; as she left the room, Ralph Bierce turned to his men saying —

"Miss Blout is above suspicion; to save a scene, we will allow her the undisturbed seclusion of her own room."

And the search began; up stairs, down stairs; from the crannies in the attic to the coal-hole in the basement was heard the tread of heavy feet. Stables, barns, orchard, grove and garden, were swept clean by busy, sin-blinded eyes, but nothing came of it; and the watchers in the room fronting the street saw the heated, foiled band move off towards the city.

"Why does n't Ralph go?" said Maggie, in a low voice to an elderly lady, who knelt by her side at the window; "he certainly can expect no civilities from me."

At a low tap at the door, Maggie rose and drew the bolt. Lizzie entered; this is the substance of her story: —

"The man with black whiskers had followed her from the roof to the dog-kennel, from the parlor to the servants' quarters, opening closets, stripping beds, and overturning couches until 'nothin' 'taint as 't was; but," said Lizzie, shaking with suppressed laughter, "Massa Harry'll match 'em for't, when he comes back."

"Go on, what then?" said Maggie, impatiently.

"Dey jest questioned me and Jake all to pieces, but we did n't know nothin'."

"Jake, here? to-day," asked Maggie.

"Yes, missis, he followed de men har."

"Well, what did you do after the men left, Lizzie?"

"I stole out to whar de sick man lay, and found him as comfortable like, as if he had n't no enemy in de world; and de little boy neber looked handsomer, den I saw him dar, playing wid two owlets, he'd found in de nest ober his head."

"Thank heaven! they are safe as yet," said Maggie.

Her companion made no remark, but behind her glasses great tears gathered, but were not allowed to fall. Brave, suffering mother, only trust, and the sorrows and pangs of earth's night shall be exchanged for the eternal day, and the crown, which even now angel hands are twining for the faithful, that endure unto the end.

CHAPTER XVI.

A STORM AND ITS EFFECTS.

The hall-bell sounded; Lizzie answered the summons, and returned saying, "Massa Bierce wanted missis."

"Insufferable! monstrous! is he not satisfied with searching my house! go back, Lizzie, and tell Ralph Bierce, your mistress will receive, through her servant, any message he has to deliver; but stay, I know Ralph's nature so well, my refusing to see him will only delay his departure. I will go this once," she said rising, "and mind, Lizzie, open this door to no one but your mistress. Ann will attend me."

On descending, she met Ralph in the hall; he was coldly polite, as before; but it required a masterly control of her feelings to retain the haughty indifference she assumed, while listening to his account of the fruitless search, when she heard him declare, with perfect nonchalance, his determination to take up his abode in her spacious house. "The situation," he said, "was the most desirable the country round for himself and men; it afforded greater facilities for perfecting their plans, than any other, which could be found."

Maggie knew that his gaze was upon her; that he was trying to read her very soul, and, with almost superhuman effort, she checked every expression, in word or look, which might betray her trepidation and intense indignation. "Her house to be made a den of robbers!" she thought, — "her presence to be polluted by the leader of a gang of men tainted with treason, whose souls crime had darkened until they were blacker than the smoke of the homes their hands had fired! I cannot suffer this outrage," and she remembered the promise she had made Harry. "Vengeance is mine," — "I will be a father to the fatherless," came to her throbbing heart; her hand dropped to her side, and she grew calm and firm; raising her eyes to Ralph's face, she said —

"This house is dear to me; it is sanctified by my parents' lives; dying they bequeathed it to me; before it shall become the rendezvous of lawless men, I will lay it in ashes, and go with my servants into the woods; and upon you, Ralph Bierce, shall rest the vengeance of a God, whose protecting care is the orphan's."

"Cousin Margaret, you mistake my meaning; it is my intention to be here certain hours of the day, and the nights, of course; there are buildings near, for my men: and I can promise you, no depredations shall be perpetrated by them; on the contrary, they will be very efficient aid in protecting your property from the predatory excursions of runaways, who infest the woods below." Then, speaking more deliberately, — "I should certainly regret seeing this fine house in ruins, but should not hesitate to raze it to the ground myself, should it prove an asylum for traitors, such as Richard Whedden or the murderer of Bill White."

"And do you, who have shot down unarmed men in the street, and followed up your persecutions with fire and insults the cruelest, come with unwashen hands to my door and cry aloud for more victims! If my house were an asylum for such, think you I would give them up? Never! I would fight for them, with them, until these rooms flowed with our blood."

"See to it, Margaret, that you hold your house free from proscribed heads; and keep such sentiments to yourself, or your life will answer for it," Ralph said; and he turned upon his heel and left the house.

"Oh! if Harry were only here!" sighed Maggie, as she ascended the stairs. "Ralph looked strangely at me; can it be that his penetrating eyes read my inmost thoughts! how strange he should have mentioned this White affair, — he will come back! — oh! what will become of us?" and she rested her aching head upon the balustrade, as if her resolute spirit fainted within her. Suddenly she thought, "I have Dr. Hall to consult, why need I fear?" and with a bounding step she gained her chamber door. On being admitted, with forced gayety she exclaimed —

"All right as yet, dear Mrs. Fay, (the name, cap, spectacles, and dress assumed, making the hunted mother a nice-looking elderly lady,) — come now and help me to uncage my bird."

The two approaching the dressing-room, tapped gently, and, at gruff tones of welcome, entered, to find Dr. Hall well armed, and complacently whiling away the tedium of solitary confinement with his meerschaum.

While Maggie related the events of the past two hours, he nodded most approvingly; but when she repeated the conversation held with Ralph, he burst in: "Who in the —— plays us false? there's a spy among us! call up the niggers! let me catch the culprit, and I'll skin him alive!

"Pomp, Lizzie, and Ann are all I have here now, and they are as true as steel," Maggie said.

"There's mischief in one of them, call them up! I say, call them up! But what's this?" raising the curtain, "rain, by my soul! Look here, a storm is on us! — to the swamp! all hands of you! he's a dead man if he gets a soaking."

Too late! the storm was already upon them, for, when they reached the hall door the rain fell in torrents.

"Stay here!" cried the doctor to the hesitating group; "when I want you, I will signal from the tree; the storm is a mad one, but it will soon spend itself." Then wrapping his rubber cape about him, he sprung with flying leaps towards the garden. They saw him reach the grove beyond, then the blinding rain shut him from view.

The blankets were folded and laid ready for use; the servants bidden to keep strict watch for signals from the swamp, and then Maggie, placing the arm of her friend within her own, drew her gently into the hall, saying —

"Let us be patient; such a storm cannot last long; brave little Percy can weather it, I know."

"Not of my child, but of the sick man I am thinking," was the rejoinder; "it would be dreadful to have him prostrated by fever again; and he is so exposed."

"Only until Dr. Hall reaches there," said Maggie, cheerfully, "his rubber cape can quite cover the nest, and keep them all as dry as bob-o-link's nestlings under his feathery coat. We will sit here, and while we are watching the storm, I will tell you what a nice nest that is, and what two old birds own it. Beyond the grove is the swamp, which separates Mr. Whedden's grounds from these. Once Cousin Harry, while hunting, quite lost himself in that almost impenetrable growth of reeds and underbrush, and only after severe labor, succeeded in reaching a cleared place. There an immense sweet gum-tree towered, and by its side was a pine. Some twenty feet from the ground these trees locked trunks, and mingled their boughs, forming a hollow capable of holding two persons comfortably. Harry has had a path cleared through the swamp so circuitously, I would defy any one, without a pilot, to find it. In our nest, (Harry and I claim it,) that is in the bosom of the sweet gum and pine, Pomp laid Mr. Whedden; and there, too, is Percy, who, Pomp said, laughed at our vine ladder and climbed the pine like a cat. But see," she added, rising, "the clouds are lifting; we shall soon see signs from the exiles;" and the two stepped out on the veranda.

True, the rain was falling slowly, and bright patches of blue were seen overhead; but the black clouds piling in the south, which they did not see, foretokened a storm fiercer than the one just passing away.

There were no signals; and by night a tempest raged. Objects, within the house and without, were whitened by the blinding light; while thunder-claps, the raging wind, and sounding rain held each heart hushed and awed.

"Every room, which faces the swamp, is brilliantly lighted; they shall see that we are thinking of them," whispered Maggie, as she turned from the door and bent over the chair in which Mrs. Fay sat, with her head bowed upon her hands.

A flash, followed by a startling clap, told those fear-smitten hearts that something near the house had been struck.

"On the lawn! missis," cried Lizzie, and Maggie followed her servant to the hall door.

Up shot the fierce flames about a grand old oak not fifty yards from the house.

"That shot was a fair one," growled the storm-king to his swarming hosts, whose panting breath tossed golden streamers and banners of dazzling light aloft; "one more charge and the revel is done." Another thunderbolt smote near, and a light beyond the grove drew the household to the east veranda.

Red, bright, and fierce rose the rioting flames, seeming to lick the thunderous concave overhead.

"The sweet gum!" groaned Maggie, and she turned in speechless agony to the mother.

CHAPTER XVII.

THE PATIENT AND BOY SAVED.

"Not so near! not so near! missis, call your boy!" "Percy! dear Percy! where are you?" but no answer came; the flames crackled and roared, and the cry was lost.

"Dey are in de canes, no signs of dem har."

Yes, for the mother's eye has caught something; she darts amid a shower of blazing sticks, and springs back unharmed. A small singed cap she presses to her lips, while tears pour down her cheeks. "See, a paper!" she cries, and she unpins the scorched scrap from within the cap.

"We are safe; come to the ———," she reads, then a fierce gust whirls the paper from her trembling hand; it is drawn towards the flames; again the fearless woman springs upon the burning fagots, but reaches her arms in vain. "It is gone!" she cries, as all ablaze it was whirled aloft, and fell, senseless.

An hour before midnight two men appear approaching the house, bearing a *third;* Lizzie and Ann follow, carrying a happy smiling mother, who holds her boy by the hand. Though her limbs are badly blistered, she heeds them not; for her heart is overflowing with joy, that the lost are found. She smiles bravely as the doctor dresses the fierce burns, and, when on leaving, he takes her hand and calls her a brave woman, a tear is on his cheek. "A cold in head," he mutters, and dashes his hand across his face.

Ah! no. Not a cold in the head, kind soul, for that was pity's tear, which so noble a heart as yours, Dr. Felix Hall, need not be ashamed to own.

"Now, Maggie," he said, when the two stood on the steps out in the night, "I shall call in during the day to pay my respects to your cousin Ralph. I have sounded Pomp and the women, they are all right; but there is a wolf somewhere; mind you keep your eyes open, and we'll track him before another day is gone."

"Ralph, doctor," sighed Maggie, "do you think he will be here to-morrow?"

"To-morrow, child, that he will, and by sunrise too. I know the man well; we have to thank the storm for preventing his return to-night.

"You think there is no danger of his attempting to force my room?"

"None now, whatever. I would not trust him this morning, but he has shown himself less keen than I thought him; we are more than a match for the scoundrel. By the way, Frank McGowan has reached home; he writes me he shall be in our city to-day."

"So soon? Harry thought it probable he would not be allowed to return."

"It was a hazardous thing any way, this journey of his; he went North for his sister, did n't he?"

"Yes. Annie McGowan has been at school in New York for several years; I shall insist upon

Frank's making his home here, while he is in the city; his presence will, in some measure, reconcile me to Ralph's infamous intrusion."

"A capital suggestion!" cried the doctor, gleefully, "I'll meet Frank at the station and send him here; next to Harry Blout, Maggie, you could not have a wiser or a cooler head to consult with; he's a man after my own heart, firm and true as steel."

Dr. Hall was right. Before breakfast was served, a clattering of hoofs was heard on the drive, and, as Maggie turned to the window, she saw Ralph and two of his men in the act of dismounting, and sighing deeply, she left the room.

Some hours later she sent for Ralph to meet her in the parlor; and on his appearance, after a few commonplace remarks, with a forced smile she asked, "if he had any choice of rooms?" The smile vanished, however, when he replied —

"The one front, which you objected to my entering yesterday, would suit my purpose best."

"That room is mine; it will remain so," Maggie replied.

"Very well. I will occupy the one opposite; the view is, perhaps, equally as good."

"That one I have reserved for Mr. McGowan, a gentleman I expect here to-day."

"Excuse me, I understood you to ask if I had a choice; it is restricted to what you have not already appropriated, I see. However, a room is of small moment; you spoke of Mr. McGowan; is it Frank McGowan of Whiteville?"

"The same," Maggie said, more eagerly than she was conscious of.

"Is he a relative?"

"A distant one; although I call him cousin."

"A valued friend? perhaps."

"Yes. Do you know him?"

"I know somewhat of him, and can safely say he will not be here to-day."

"Why?"

"I read in this morning's paper, that a man, answering to such a name, was arrested last evening, while on his way to this city, for expressing sentiments decidedly obnoxious to his travelling companions. The paper did not state what, but it seems enough was said to have him passed up the road to Salisbury."

At this moment Maggie was called from the room. With her usual grace she crossed the long parlor; but the hall gained, and that stabbing voice lost to her tortured senses, she could restrain her feelings no longer.

"Anything, Lizzie," she whispered, "only leave me undisturbed for an hour."

Lizzie looked into her mistress' face and forbore to make her request. She saw her enter the library; then clinching her huge hand she shook it before the open parlor door, muttering —

"Yer'll kill 'er! yer old sarpent, if Massa Harry stays up yonder many more days! but I've swared to save her, and old black Liz. will do it!"

CHAPTER XVIII.

INTRODUCING NEW CHARACTERS.

INTO one of the few handsome residences which grace the antiquated town of Whiteville, let me transport you, reader. The house and its surroundings bespeak wealth, and the cultivated taste of the owner. Our attention, however, is drawn to the two persons who sit busily sewing upon the veranda.

The elder is a noble-looking lady of some forty years; her face is expressive of goodness and beauty; her eyes are full and earnest, and her smile, irresistibly winning. Those who knew Mrs. McGowan most intimately, wondered how one bred in an atmosphere of pride and ultra refinement, could, so unreservedly, associate with the less favored ones, among whom, in later years, her lot was cast. It was the Christian loveliness of her character, which endeared her alike to all, even the most prejudiced of her neighbors, who, on her advent among them, declared — "They had no use for aristocratic Virginians; too fine ladies for their town; for all they could see they were as good as she, if not quite as ladyish," &c., &c.

The young girl at her side is her daughter; she has the same full eye and wavy brown hair; her features are regular, with a liveliness of expression, which portrays every change of feeling.

"Do see! mamma," she exclaimed petulantly, "how this thread will knot; if I were sewing for the Yankees, my needle would go as smoothly as Aunt Lucy's shuttle."

"You would be less troubled, my daughter, if you would take more interest in your work, and not keep your eyes on the road so intently."

"Nothing ever came of an attempt to accomplish a thing the heart does not sanction; so good by homespun; some one else will have to sew for Jeff. Davis's soldiers, I can't longer."

Annie tossed her work into her maid's lap, and, springing to her feet, clapped her hands for her pony, capering near. His attention caught, she pointed at the post, where the saddle hung, then at the coachman. Away trotted the docile creature, and taking the saddle between his teeth bore it to the stable and laid it carefully down at the groom's feet.

"Quick! John," shouted the little lady, "and do you saddle the mare and accompany me." Then dropping her voice, she thus soliloquized: —

"Once in the woods and I can sing 'Red, White, and Blue,' and 'John Brown,' to my heart's content. Mamma has never heard the latter; I believe I will surprise her with one stanza."

Annie's voice was of singular sweetness and rare compass; and the verse was sung with such effect, as to draw many an ebon face from tasks assigned. With "Glory, Glory, Hallelujah" still on her lip, she turned to note the effect of tabooed patriotism upon her mother, when, to her great discomfiture, she discerned one of their neighbors approaching.

Thinking to escape observation she bent low behind some flowering shrubs near, whispering to herself: "If there is n't old lady Prue! I do wonder what she comes here for; it was only last week she said the McGowans were all Yankees and ought to be put in jail;—despicable secesh! I wish such as you would stay away from those you affect to despise!"

"Annie," said her mother; but the young girl was too intent with her own plans, for the most consistent treatment to be tendered an avowed enemy, to heed; at the second bidding, however, she arose and walked deliberately up to the caller in the deep fly-bonnet.

"How do you do? Mrs. Prue," she said, extending her hand.

"How d'y, Miss Ann? I'm tolerable, are you well?"

"Quite so; and your family?"

"Are all up, I believe."

The usual salutatory remarks over, Annie seated herself where she could escape her mother's eye and any gestures she might make by way of caution.

Mrs. Prue, at her hostess' request, laid aside the fly-bonnet, and drew her hoopless skirts about her; then, as her custom was, took from her pocket a small tin box and brush.

"Have a dip, Mrs. McGowan? May be you have a brush of your own."

"Thank you, Mrs. Prue, but I never dip." *

---

* This custom of dipping is almost universal at the South,— high and low, rich and poor, mistress and slave, practise it. The slave makes the brush for her mistress by chewing a little twig of a certain kind of wood, until the end is like a fine soft brush.

"But, Miss Ann, you will!" and the gill of macaboy was extended to the right.

"I have n't any brush," said Annie, with well-feigned regret.

"I suppose you would n't use mine?"

"My daughter never dips," Mrs. McGowan quietly remarked.

"Well! well! neither of you dip? It's a mighty fortunate thing these days. Snuff is growing so high; it's a dollar a pound now, and hard to get at that. What we are all coming to, if the Yankees dont stop this fuss soon, I can't for the life of me tell."

"The destruction which threatens, is appalling, certainly."

"Yes, Mrs. McGowan, bread and meat may be scarce; money, however, will purchase food, and you and I have nothing to fear on that score; but laws-a-me! *snuff*, it can't be had in the Southern Confederacy two months longer! It is bread and meat to me, and it's something I can't do without."

"Have you sent to our larger cities for it?"

"Yes, everywhere in the State, but it can't be had," said Mrs. Prue, most despondingly.

"Why not grind up tobacco and put salt with it? our niggers do so;" said Annie.

"Why, child, it would be strong enough to start every tooth in my head! I have fifteen pounds laid by, but that much will not last three weeks, — three weeks! no! for Clara and Sallie are inveterate dippers, like myself; and then the niggers steal at least a quarter of a pound a week."

"Jane, bring a spittoon," her mistress said.

It is then given to her mistress, who hides it under her garter, ready for use.

"Never mind, Mrs. McGowan, I can clear the steps. I never soil my own;" but the spittoon was brought, and Mrs. McGowan was spared further exhibition of her guest's proficiency in "clearing steps."

"Miss Ann, you were singing a beautiful tune as I came up," said Mrs. Prue, graciously, "you did n't learn that up North, I'm sure."

"Glory, Glory, Hallelujah, was that it?" and Annie hummed the first line.

"Yes, yes, that's it; it's a grand old Methodist psalm tune; let me hear it again."

Without waiting to be urged, Annie sang one verse of the song.

"There, that's what I call good music, *real* soul-stirring," cried the delighted lady. "I must have my girls learn it; but who was this Ellsworth? He must have been a mighty good man, to have had such a song as that made up about him."

"So he was, Mrs. Prue, and has gone to glory, you may be sure," said the young girl, reverently.

"I don't doubt it, my dear; but is that all of the tune?"

"There is another verse about a martyr John, whom, 't is said, *wise* men slew."

"It's good, I know, sing that," but a cough from her mother warned the now laughing girl that she must go no farther.

"I cannot work and sing too," she replied. "You must excuse me from music until I have finished my afternoon's task?"

"Afternoon! there, that's one of the Yankee words which provokes the girls so to hear; they tell me, Miss Ann, you are a Yankee all over. I did n't believe it though; but I thought I'd come and see. You have n't had many callers since you come home, I reckon."

"The misses of her age have not been to see her," said Mrs. McGowan.

"No, and, they say, they wont come until she has dropped them Yankee airs she has; but for my part, I can't see but she appears just the same as if she had n't been up to New York."

"I am sure if Annie's young mates should visit her, they would find her no more changed than you and I."

"They see her at church, they say, and that's enough for them; them pink roses on the top of her bonnet and on the inside too, they hate, they are so Yankeeish; there is n't a girl around here, little or big, who would wear them. So, Miss Ann, if you want the girls to visit you, you must leave off such miserable finery, and do as they do."

"How is that?" Annie asked, in so subdued a tone that the zealous neighbor was encouraged to administer more wholesome advice.

"Why, take off your hoops, and wear your old bonnet and old frocks, as all of *us* have sworn to do; yes, (more vehemently) *sworn* to deny ourselves everything of the kind, *all from principle*, you see, until this war is over; just to match Northern shop-keepers, for sending their clerks down here to steal our niggers. They'll learn, too late, whose money they've been living on! But we've shut our purses *now*, and never, never will buy or use another article of Yankee make; nor would you, Miss Ann, if you had the right kind of principle about you." Mrs. McGowan was at this moment called into the house.

Annie arose, and taking her mother's chair at the side of Mrs. Prue, said —

"I am quite sure that I can convince you I am a girl of some principle. See, here are clothes I am making for the soldiers; now, there's industry in my favor, is n't there?"

"Why, yes; but one must do something besides making soldier's clothes, if they would stop the war."

"I am making a red, white, and blue flag; there's patriotism for my list."

"What are you making *three* flags for, child?"

"I am not making three flags, only one; *our* flag, which is red, white, and blue."

"Three colors in one flag?"

"Certainly; it's an old saying, that those three colors properly put together, make a banner which no tyrant can see without trembling."

"Why, you don't say so!" ejaculated the astonished lady. "I'll tell Clara and Sal about it; they 've been making a flag out of red bunting, but it can't be half so handsome as yours; you will let us see it when it is done, won't you?"

"Yes; you shall see it just before I give it to the soldiers it is made for; you will want one like it *then*."

"I dare say I shall. I declare, I'd like to see a flag, which would bring them horrid Yankees down on their knees; for if they ar n't tyrants, there are no tyrants in the world."

"Mrs. Prue," said Annie, solemnly, "it's my opinion, that if you and I live long enough, we shall see every one in these States of America under this flag."

"The good Lord grant it!"

"Amen!" was Annie's fervent response.

"But, Annie, what name do you give it?"

"Columbia's flag; it's a pretty name, don't you think so?"

"Yes; but it's a right smart hard one to remember."

"Never mind the *name*, that is nothing; it is what is done under it, which makes us proud of it."

"That is my idea, exactly."

"Now, one word about fashions," said the mischievous girl, demurely; "you tell your daughters that they can wear their hoops, and the very nicest things they can find in our stores; for the styles have changed so much since our merchants went North, no one here can be accused of imitating Northern fashions, let them dress as they will."

"You are sure of that, are you? for my girls would die, before they would wear the first thing like them miserable Yankees."

"Yes, quite sure; just to look at Godey's last fashion plates—"

"Have you Godey's last?" and the neighbor's chair approached the settee where Annie sat, moderately fast. "How I should like to take one, just one little look into it; Clara and Sallie are dying for Godey, but there! they would n't touch it, nor Harper and Frank Leslie's trash *now*, for their weight in gold! But I might get some little idea how to fix up their bonnets and frocks for summer (they would n't know it, you know), they do look so shabby! It would n't be *helping* the North any if I looked out of *your* book, would it?"

"Yes, Mrs. Prue; you might look into my book,

to be sure, but I have too much principle to tempt any one to sacrifice *truth*, or to pilfer what they openly scoff at," and the young girl raised her earnest eyes to the face, which was bent down to her box, in which the mop was twirling with unusual rapidity.

"Steal, child, steal!" said the slightly disconcerted neighbor, clearing her mouth, in a manner more decorously imagined than described, for a fresh dip, "I feel we have thrown away a great deal of money upon Northern trash, Northern humbuggery, and it is my *due* to make it up when I can. There is one comfort, though, we are done with them and their lies now and forever! It is a very serious matter to the Yankees, however, very serious; husband says, — and he ought to know, for he has been North every year for goods except this last one, — he says, the North must burst up completely without our trade; and what's more, he says thousands will die in the streets for the corn we throw to our hogs. The vengeance of God is upon them for their sins, so every minister in the land will tell you."

CHAPTER XIX.

PREPARING FOR THE BALL.

"SEE my beautiful pony, Mrs. Prue!" exclaimed Annie, interrupting the story of Northern destruction which she had heard, not once, but scores of times during the short two weeks she had been at home, "is n't 'he a beauty with his new saddle on? it is a Spanish saddle; I brought it with me from New York."

"Then, for the Lord's sake, don't ask me to admire it!" was the indignant reply. "Who do you suppose will ask you to ride with *that thing* on your horse? And that reminds me, the gentlemen here have sworn not to notice a lady, be she young or old, who has n't on a secesh badge; and the ladies also have bound themselves by an oath to frown down, to cut completely, every man who refuses to volunteer; that's my spirit, exactly. Yankee sympathizers can't live here!"

"Are Clara and Sallie going to the ball?" asked Annie, seemingly too intent upon the antics of her pony, to notice the look Mrs. Prue favored her with, as she uttered her last emphatic words.

"To be sure they are;—they are among the managers."

"Then the ladies invite?"

"Of course they do; I suppose you did n't expect an invitation?"

"I have received none."

"No indeed! there is n't a dozen, no, not half that number, who would go if you were to be there. Your brother Frank's not volunteering has set people to talking awfully about you all; if Frank knew what was good for himself, he would fall into the ranks before he is a day older."

"Brother Frank is not a man to be intimidated into doing anything," was the emphatic reply; then, after a short pause, — "but do tell me, what the girls will wear to-morrow night?"

"Oh, dear! that's what troubles the whole of us — (and still more despondingly) their pink silks are badly faded and their muslins wretchedly torn. They are worried to death nearly, for fear they shall not look as well as the rest."

"How cheap silks were selling, when I bought mine," said Annie, absently; "the nicest kind for a dollar a yard; fortunately I laid in a supply of thread, needles, pins, shoes, and frocks of various kinds. Why, they told me at the store, yesterday, that in less than a month not a thing of the kind could be had in the market."

"Yes, indeed, that's so. Not a pin, nor a spool of thread can be had here, to-day, nor this side of Newbern. I sent Dick there, this morning, and if there are none to be had in that city, the girls will have to stay at home from the ball, and it will well-nigh kill them to do that."

"If they have nothing new to make up, what need have they of thread?"

"Why, child, if they do not wear hoops they

must tuck up their skirts. They could n't dance with them laying two feet on the floor, could they?"

"They had better wear their hoops then."

"That's very well said; but, to be honest about it, they have n't got any to wear; theirs are all broken up, and there are none to be had to replace them."

"I have three; but they are of the very newest style."

"Yes, we all saw yours last Sunday. It sets your dress out awfully about the bottom; but if that's the fashion, no matter;" up came the chair and the capped head dropped again to the girl's blooming face; "Look here, Miss Ann, rather than have the girls stay at home and lose such a ball, — a real soldier's ball, — the first one we have ever had here, you know, maybe, if Dick brings no pins nor thread, I'll slip round or send one of the niggers and borrow a hoop for each of the girls; they need n't know but Dick brought them from Newbern."

Again Annie's face assumed a very grave expression as she said, "No, Mrs. Prue, they will never know anything about it, for it would be unprincipled in me to lend my hoops, or anything else which has been condemned, or to help cheat anybody."

A small cough, another dip, and Mrs. Prue arose to go, saying, — "Of course, of course, you can do as you please. If the girls, however, have anything which you would like to borrow, don't hesitate to send round, I like to be on good terms with all my neighbors; and tell your mother," she added, drawing on her fly-bonnet, "she must come round and see us; and you must come too, Miss Ann, when you can feel and act as every Southern Christian should."

She turned to leave, when, stopping suddenly as a young lady rode up to the gate, she exclaimed, "If there is n't Puss Smith! I should n't think *she* would come here!"

"Dear Annie, I have just got home myself, or I should have been here before," were the words Mrs. Prue heard, as, with her bosom rife with enmity and rankling jealousy, she turned from the gate to tread the sandy road homeward.

A twofold object had this neighbor in view, when she announced to her astonished family circle her intention to call upon the McGowans: the first, and most essential, she thought to accomplish by going through the garden, thinking to hear something " on the sly," which *she* could hurl into the unquiet stream of conflicting rumors, whose black waves of error and exaggeration were so soon to engulf that cheerful and devoted home: the other, to obtain a piece of Yankee finery, and, with such adventitious aid, to "fine" her girls for the ball; and in both endeavors, we have seen, she met with signal failure. As Mrs. Prue passes from sight, feeling as uncomfortable, inly, as the evil-disposed can feel, when the heart, expanding to embrace some cherished project, is made to contract sharply under the stab of mortifying defeat, — our best wishes that she may reach a happier goal than the one she is now heading for, attend her.

"Why, Annie, the sun has set," said her companion, jumping up. "Who would have thought I had been here two hours and more! But there, I cannot leave until I know what you will wear at the ball to-morrow night."

"I have had no invitation to attend the ball," and

Annie repeated Mrs. Prue's remarks, adding, "I do not care to go; I have said I would not wear those secesh badges, and I will not!"

"Annie McGowan, now hear me. I am head manager of this ball; your name I have seen upon the list of guests, and your brother's also, although great opposition was offered to his being invited. Why your invitation has not been sent, is something for me to find out. Did Mrs. Prue's 'girls,' as she calls them, dare to erase your names during my absence? I think not, but I will investigate this matter thoroughly, and see to whom this neglect is chargeable. The girls around here, from what I hear, are envious of you, solely because you have more stylish clothes than they, and look so beautifully in them, too."

"It is better for me not to meet with them, then, if, as you say, my presence excites envy."

"No such thing, Annie dear. Now promise me you will go to-morrow night, and wear the most stylish clothes you have: then I must be off."

"I cannot promise, for papa and Frank are both away, and I would not like to leave mamma alone."

"Only say you will go," pleaded the young lady, "and I will find your mother a companion. You know we have a nice chatty aunt living with us; now she will be delighted to spend an evening here, to ventilate some of her odd notions about this war; say you will go, and brother aud I will call for you in the carriage."

Annie finally gave her consent to the arrangement, and then followed a long discussion upon dress and ball-adornings. Miss Smith's wardrobe, as described by herself, kept her young friend in a right merry mood and constantly repeating, "it can't be half as bad! you surely do exaggerate!"

"Well, if you distrust what I say, come and see for yourself." Then, with her face flushed with mortification, and her heart fired with bitter animosity towards the supposed author of her riches in rags, the excited girl stamped her foot upon the floor, exclaiming —

"Abe Lincoln shall yet pay for all these annoyances, all this scrimping and pulling to keep one's self decently clothed! You must know, Annie, we are to march from Washington on to New York, and from there, who can tell where? What folly it is for our people to say, we have no use for the North; now I would just like to know who cares a fig for a bonnet, or a garment of any kind, unless it comes from New York? It's the Yankees, themselves, we can do without, but not their splendid cities; to think of our owning Washington, New York, Saratoga, and Newport! Imagine, if you can, our walking into Stewart's, Ball & Black's, and Tiffany's, and taking what we want without as much as, 'by your leave.' It is wicked for me to grumble about a frock *now*, when in a month, or six weeks at the latest, we half-starved, half-nude Dixieites shall have

> Gowans of silk and golden ore,
> Evermore, evermore!

Fortunate it is indeed for us, that we are of the right age to enjoy such conquests!"

"What news have you, Miss Mary?" asked Mrs. McGowan, stepping out on the veranda and seating herself beside the young girls. "Do to-day's telegrams bring what is favorable to our arms?"

"O, Mrs. McGowan, I have heard no particular news; I have only been fitting a key to the lock our soldiers are to turn."

"And what is the treasure so ponderous a lock withholds?"

"Liberty."

"What do you mean by that, Mary?"

"To do just what one wants to do, and in a way it suits one best; *that's* what *I* call liberty; and 'tis what we have known as little about, under Yankee rule, as those nigs yonder."

"How are we to get such unconditional power, if you mean by us, the South?"

"Why, by whipping the North, as we are going to do at Manassas."

"Our soldiers are confident of victory, I know; but we must remember that those who stand arrayed against us, are powerful."

"As to numbers, yes; but when we have God on our side, what good will men and money do them?"

"Are we sure we have the God of battles on our side?"

"Certainly, for God always favors the right; and I am equally sure, that that rich Astor's money might as well be thrown into the sea, as to be handed over to Abe Lincoln. Just to think of one man giving a hundred million to prosecute this war, and promising to lend as many more! Uncle James says, those merchant princes of New York are made of gold; and we all know, *now*, that what has been said of their being so grasping and mercenary as to sell their own children for a sixpence, is too true."

Mrs. McGowan cast an anxious, warning glance upon her daughter; she saw that her cheek was flushed, and it was with difficulty she could restrain her emotions. She waited until her passion had subsided, and then said: —

"I have heard you speak often of Mr. Astor's wealth, Annie. Can't you set your young friend right as regards a true estimate of his property? I saw the statement of his enormous wealth in our paper; but I am sure, although a very rich man, Mr. Astor has not so many millions to give Mr. Lincoln, or any one else."

But the young lady was not to be convinced. "She should believe the papers, the Southern papers, before any assertion Northerners might make."

Annie yielded the point with a good-natured laugh, and her friend coming off conqueror, continued her storm of invective against the North, until words were exhausted, if her passion was not, and finished by extolling the efficiency of Southern troops and their ability to annihilate any force which might be sent down upon them, from North, East, and West.

"My dear young friend," said Mrs. McGowan, "you must not be too sanguine; the wail of defeat may yet sound throughout our young Confederacy. The North and South are one people; the valor, fidelity, and endurance shown by one faction may be equally matched by the other. We must be prepared for any event which may happen; remember great deeds are not always the sons of mighty resolutions."

"How little your mother knows about the Yankees," said Puss Smith, as Mrs. McGowan's footsteps were lost in the distance. "Defeat, indeed!

there's not a Southern soldier but would die twice, before he would run from, or suffer himself to be taken prisoner by a Yankee! What can a set of Yankee mechanics do, when face to face with *our* men, strong and brave as lions! Why, of course, they will run, — run with lightning speed too, to their coal-hods, mallets, and spades, where they came from. Let the North send her *gentlemen* into the field, as the South has to do, then we shall see fair combat; but their fine men stay at home twirling their moustaches and smoking their meerschaums, while the scum of their cities is hurled into Dixie, to pollute her homes, to say to Southern chivalry, "Take up the hoe and dig with us, — you have played the gentleman long enough, — Abe Lincoln has other use for your niggers! I say, Annie, it is nigger's work to fight such, — and let niggers take the field!"

"Who'll gather the crops, Puss, if we turn our negroes into soldiers?"

"There's white trash enough for such labor."

"But you know, as well as I, they will not do nigger's work."

"They can be starved to it."

"Puss," said Annie lowering her voice, "do you want to see arms in our negroes hands? Are we sure they would fight *for* us, if they thought by fighting against us, they would be free?"

"Why, Annie, how foolishly you talk! Just as though they would dare to turn against us, while we hold their women and children!"

"And if the North should say, "Come over to us, and we will free your women and children," what then?"

"I wish the North had them,— every soul of them," said Puss, musingly, and then with more energy,— "I have heard papa say, time and again, he wished slavery could be done away with, that niggers were a torment, eating and destroying in one year more than they are worth; and, for my part, I am heartily sick of them, they are so mean."

"But say, Puss, what would you do, if they *should* all run off?— you, who have never raised a finger to help yourself."

"I, a waiting-maid, compelled to handle a broom, to hook my frock, and lace my boots,— never!" said Puss, emphatically.

"Why not? We may all have to come to that."

"No, indeed, my little Yankee sympathizer! You forget, if the time should come, which sees smutty faces, little and big, gathered into the bosom of Abraham's family, we shall have prisoners to fill their places; they will only be too glad to exchange ball and chain, for hoe and spade. I do declare, I would turn overseer myself to see Yankee Doodle stepped out at the double quick, under my lash! The Yankee women, they tell me, are neat and smart as crickets; wouldn't I like a house full of them, subject to my will!" Then dropping her light, mocking tone, she continued: "Slavery is a curse,— a terrible curse! But the evil is here, and cannot be done away with in our time, and if ever,— *never* at the dictation of the North. If the negro question, as it is generally believed, is the cause of this rupture between North and South, there will be treasure and blood uselessly spent,— for the issue of this strife will be slavery still,— but in a more aggravated form than we now know it to exist."

A voice from the road at this moment shouted, "out beyond hours!" and Puss springing to her feet, exclaimed: "There's brother Jim, for me now. Not an hour after sunset is it safe to be out without proper escort, the niggers are so saucy. Oh, dear! when will this state of things end?" she added, somewhat despondingly, as the two drew near the gate; and, before she mounted her horse, she bent down to whisper: "If you should hear unpleasant things said about your brother, to-morrow night, be too sensible to mind them. If he is as rank an abolitionist as Aunt Fannie " —

"Frank is not an abolitionist," said Annie, indignantly interrupting her.

"He is called so because he will not volunteer, and is accused of keeping others from doing so. I do hope he will not fall into his Uncle Calvin's power."

"Brother knows how to take care of himself," was the rejoinder, and the young friends parted.

CHAPTER XX.

IGNORANCE AND HATRED.

"Mamma," said Annie, as mother and daughter sat together in the deepening twilight, "what a comfort it is to be alone; we have scarcely had an hour to ourselves since my return. Curiosity, we know, brings the greater part of our visitors to the house, and I must say I have no patience with them; for not a third part of the people about here read a newspaper, but credit every idle story which is afloat."

"Annie, there would be no merit in cultivating patience in our hearts, if there was nothing to bear; nor to bear cheerfully, if there was nothing to endure; trials make our faith perfect."

"But, mamma, how can one as hot-tempered as myself have patience with people, who, like dogs, swallow the bone the master flings at them, whether it is poison or not? I told Mr. Wilson, who rode up soon after Puss Smith left, of my conversation with one of our neighbors on our flag. He laughed heartily and said, the men in the gross were no better informed; he had himself, within a month, proposed as a toast the 'Red, white, and blue,' to a crowd who had been railing at and cursing the supporters of that very flag, and it was drunk with prolonged cheers.* I do not wonder at such ignorance in an old lady like Mrs. Prue, who has no thought, no aspiration aside from what money can bring; but for men to be so grossly ignorant as to curse and cheer the same flag in the same breath, is almost incredible. No marvel that Calvin Hicks and his party, under false pretences, swell their ranks with thousands of such dupes. I hope to see the day their eyes are opened, and they are fully conscious of the game Jeff. Davis and his tools make of them."

"Be careful, Annie, that you do not repeat any of Mr. Wilson's remarks out of the house; he says here what he would not say elsewhere. He is a marked man, and, like your father and brother, accused of being a traitor, for declaring this war unnecessary."

Still later in the evening Annie drew to her mother's side, begging to know why her Uncle Calvin had, for years, shown such ill-will towards their family.

"What put that thought into your head to-night?" asked Mrs. McGowan, somewhat startled.

"Something which Puss Smith said on leaving, has filled my mind with Col. Hicks, (I like best to call him so, mamma,) and I have been wondering what any one of us could have done or said, to have made him such an enemy."

"It is a sad, sad story, my daughter, and a trial to me to fill your young heart with the sinfulness of an uncle, and that uncle my only brother. But," she resumed with a sigh, "it is, perhaps, well that

---

* This may appear almost incredible to Northerners, but is none the less a fact, for I had it from the gentleman himself, beside others of a similar nature. It is *this ignorance* that gives the leaders of this Rebellion their power. — AUTHOR.

you should know what the world knows; that in your daily supplication at the throne of grace, you may evoke God's mercy to the healing of a soul corrupt with a long-continued course of sin. Calvin, when a boy, was headstrong and passionate, and the cause of great anguish to our parents. I was the only one who exercised any control over him, and never entirely lost my influence, until his shameful, profligate life made me close my doors upon him, and discard his image wholly from my heart. His wife died here, you remember. When she fled from the persecutions of the slave, who had usurped the authority, privilege, and affection of the wife, I took her home. But her days were few; we soon laid her side by side with the beautiful babes God had given, but in his mercy removed, before the sin of their father had tainted their young lives. Twice Calvin and your father were rival candidates for the same office; your father's success, and my meddling with his domestic affairs, as he called it, is the cause of the relentless animosity he has shown towards us all. He leaves, however, with his regiment the day after to-morrow; then, I hope, your father and brother will be spared the contumely which, as non-combatants, he has neglected no opportunity to heap upon them."

"I will not go to the ball, mamma, for I am sure I shall meet him there."

"No indeed, Annie, he has no taste for such gayeties. It is my wish that you should go; if you are the good-natured girl there you are at home, I am sure your companions will forget the prejudice they have conceived against you. If annoyed by their remarks, remember the efficacy of a soft answer," she added, smoothing the brown head which had displaced the work in her lap.

"I will go, if you wish it; and if Frank prevails upon Maggie Blout to return with him, they may be here in season to attend with me."

An hour later, and a carriage was heard upon the drive. "Here they are, now!" cried Annie, springing to the door, to welcome the travellers.

"Massa Frank, did n't come," shouted John, and the carriage turned from the drive to the stable.

CHAPTER XXI.

THE REVEL — HOW IT ENDED.

> "Beautiful being in robes of white,
> The prettiest nightgowns under the sun;
> Stockingless, slipperless, sit in the night,
> For the revel is done."

"WILL they live to come back?" and the weary head of the speaker drooped sadly upon the mantle.

"Why, Carrie, of course they will. Have you forgotten Big Bethel fight?"

"If the Yankees can't hurt them, camp fever may."

"Oh, ghost of Moll Pitcher! Carrie, if you are so timorous a woman, as to scream at shadows, you are no fit mate for the Captain. By the way, how well he looked to-night, and Ned, too; the major seemed to have jumped from a nice little lover to a deity to be worshipped."

"Cousin Ned certainly never looked better; and you have rewarded him at length for his persistent devotion, Sallie?"

"Why, yes, I suppose so," and the heightened color and sparkling eye which the confession kindled; chased away the weariness which was before apparent in the heavy eyelid and sinking voice. "Now that Ned is really going away," she resumed, "I feel I shall miss him wretchedly. I have promised him, that I will keep all my songs and smiles until his return; and he has promised me, — what? Carrie, I would try your powers for divining the occult."

"To come back to claim the consummation of vows plighted."

"More than that: try again."

"Never to run from or allow himself to be taken prisoner by a Yaukee."

"Carrie!" burst in the indignant girl, "you insult your cousin! Run from a Yankee! Allow himself to be taken prisoner!" and a scornful laugh followed the mocking words. "Think you he or any other man would show himself in my presence that ever stepped a foot from the path of Yankee scavengers! *Over them,* is the road to Washington!"

Without waiting for further conjecture on the part of her companion, and with the angry flush still on her cheek, she continued, — "He has promised to come as an Indian warrior, with his wampum-belt decked with Yankee bones, to lay his trophies at my feet, — or he comes not at all, — and he is to me as though he were not."

"Monstrous!" exclaimed Carrie, while a very perceptible shudder shook her lightly-draped figure, "I hate the Yankees as much as you, Sallie, but I hate barbarity more."

"My dear, little fluttering friend, you will be the first to borrow my Yankee toys!"

"Never, Sallie Prue! Were cousin Ned, or any man I know, to perpetrate such a wicked deed as to scalp his brother man, were he twice the foe the Yankee is, I would rank and treat him too as the vilest, the most bloodthirsty savage, that ever trod the earth! And O, Sallie," she pleaded, "Edward loves you devotedly, passionately, and do you require of him a sacrifice of honor, manliness, and humanity, in order that a cruel whim may be gratified? Dare you wrest from the heart, which you have made weak as a child's, the noble attributes God has placed there, and send him out to the battle-field with the scalping-knife in his hand, and the ferocious passions of the savage within his breast?"

"You are a goosey, Carrie, to run on so about savages and scalping-knives. Everything is fair in war; and if worse than savages come out against us, tomahawk must meet tomahawk, knife meet knife."

"Sallie, how can you talk so wickedly?"

"There, Carrie, dry your tears, and I will talk of something else, lest you dream of death-heads, and prate of my depraved taste to your soldierly lord that is to be. He, by the way, is as much like you, as two tears on pity's cheek. I am sure you would both nurse a sick Yankee, as tenderly as you would one of our own soldiers. As for the Captain, — we all know he is a splendid shot, — should he bring down a dozen of these Yankees, he would as quickly throw away his gun, rush to his game, bind up wounds, wash faces, and set the blockheads again on their feet; then, with a polite bow and encouraging smile, turn back to the ranks."

"Captain Lee is a gentleman and a soldier; he knows his duty, and will do it honorably," Carrie replied. "Come now, and lie down, Sallie, we have talked long, and I am very weary."

"Not yet. You go home to-morrow; this is our

last night together, and my heart is in a flutter to relieve itself."

"Of what?"

"Of what you said in the carriage you wished I would not speak of there."

"Say on, now; there was one with us at the time, who might have been hurt by your remarks."

"Who?"

"Miss Mary Smith."

"Puss Smith? Not she, indeed! she talks about our abolition neighbors as unsparingly as myself."

"But she was the only one, to-night, who showed herself friendly to Annie McGowan."

"Were you in her set, when her Uncle Calvin accosted her so ungraciously?"

"I was directly opposite her, and was, at the very moment, admiring her bright and beautiful face, and the perfect simplicity of her dress, which so charmingly set off her youthful figure and graceful movements."

"Tell me just what she said, and how she looked, when she answered Col. Hicks."

"I saw this dark, fierce-looking Colonel when he came into the hall, and I was told afterward, that as soon as his eye rested on his niece, he stopped in his walk, and watched her through the figure. He then walked directly up to our set, and touched her upon the shoulder. Miss Annie had been laughing with her partner, Lieut. Smith, but when she turned and saw the man who confronted her, her cheek lost its beautiful color, and her girlish face at once became white and firm. When he said, 'Col. Hicks,' she bowed; it was wonderful to see how she retained her composure, when so many eyes were upon her; but she did, perfectly, even when he said, loud enough for us all to hear, 'When I left Frank at Salisbury, he gave me this,' and he handed her a slip of paper. Oh! what a fierce look he fixed on her sweet face, as she read those few words. Raising her eyes to those bent upon her, she said, 'This is your work.'

"It is my work to seize traitors, wherever I find them," he replied, sneeringly.

"Col. Hicks," she said firmly, "if you have anything more to say to me, select a more suitable place. You impede the dance." Then turning to her partner, she spoke in a low voice, and the two left the hall. With a smile which made me loathe the man, he watched her from sight; then turned on his heel, and joined a group on the rostrum.

In a few moments, the news that Frank McGowan was in prison at Salisbury, spread through the hall, and what rejoicings followed! I was glad Miss McGowan had left. It was this Miss Smith, or Puss Smith, as you call her, and her brother, who escorted her to the carriage. I afterward heard Miss Puss sharply contradict many things that were said of the McGowans, and openly declare Calvin Hicks was the fabricator of every vile story which was circulated about the family."

"Well, for my part, Carrie, I am not sorry Frank McGowan is in prison; he is no coward, I know, but those who will not come out and openly espouse our cause, must be against us, and the sooner such people are out of harm's way, the better. I am sorry that Annie should have heard such unpleasant news in the ball-room. But there, that is throwing sympathy away. The McGowans are a proud set, and, no doubt, will hold their heads as high as ever, if Frank is a jail bird. Now, to change the subject, what do you think of homespun in a ball-room?"

"I saw, a short time since, in the papers, that the belle of —— set the fashion there."

"Likely as not. We've all got to come to it, thanks to Abe Lincoln's ships."

"Yes, Sallie, homespun and brogans must soon banish silks and French slippers."

"There is one comfort, though," yawned the sleepy girl, "the gentlemen are all away; and when there is nobody to admire, who cares whether one has on French work or niggers."

CHAPTER XXII.

THE EFFECT OF THE FIGHT AT MANASSAS.

MOTHERS, wives, and sisters, with exultant hearts, had seen loved ones depart, and called down God's blessing upon the cause, which had clad their limbs with steel, and sent them forth to the strife with "*Sic semper tyrannis*" on their banners, and "Liberty" their battle-cry.

Long and weary days the fond watchers looked for glad tidings, and as they came not, the smile of exultation faded, and anxious thoughts filled the minds, and spectral shadows the hearts of the groups, which gathered in the streets, or clustered around saddened hearthstones.

The list of hospital sick and the dead, grew longer and longer, to the eyes which scanned the papers; for military discipline, severe labor, and exposure, together with the want of proper clothing and wholesome food, were fast decimating the ranks, "invulnerable to Yankee lead."

Many, who had bidden gray beards and beardless youths to the field, now, in unutterable anguish, bemoaned them dead.

"What is Washington, or New York to me?" groaned the stricken widow, as the pitying heart of some kind neighbor whispered of coming victories.

"I bid my boys go to kill the Yankees!" the childless mother shrieked, "and they have died without a shot at them!"

"If the —— Yankees don't pitch in soon," growled a fierce-looking Breckite, as his eye run down the long list, "the devil will leave none of us to"— the paper fell to the floor, while a fearful groan issued from his lips writhing in agony: "Dead! dead! John and Bill dead, and no fight yet!"

What followed, smote the mother's ear, hastening to her husband's side for news from the boys. In that mother's heart there was a love for the "Stars and Stripes," which nothing could efface; and on her knees she thanked God and wept tears of joy, that her sons had been taken before their young lives were stained with a brother's blood, — that, though they had carried the sword to cut down the noble flag, He had smitten the upraised arm, and taken the misguided ones from further contact with earth's sinfulness. "May the Lord and Giver of life protect the right," was the unceasing prayer of that Christian mother.

The long night of suspense was over. "Our loss is heavy, but our cause is won," was flashed with lightning rapidity throughout the length and breadth of the young Confederacy. Shouts and shrieks of frenzied joy rent the air. Stores were closed, houses deserted, and duties forgotten. Friend met friend, — "We are free," leaped from every eye and every tongue; while each footfall rung out a note of victory.

"Twenty thousand Yankees dead!" was the morning salute; high noon sounded "Forty thousand of the Vandals killed!" but nightfall came down with the tale: "The Grand Army of the Potomac crippled to a man! — a hundred thousand stands of arms taken! Washington deserted, — and General Scott a prisoner of the " warrior President;" who, in a hand to hand fight, had vanquished the invincible hero of the North!"

* * * * *

"Dixie forever! The North is ours!" came to the strained ears and fiercely-beating hearts, that in damp and filthy cells, at the iron-barred windows, and in deep and noisome swamps, heard.

High o'er the "Te Deum Laudamus," which came from Potomac's shore, and swelling, thundered o'er the lowlands of the Gulf, rose the piercing wail of these crushed and bleeding ones — "God have mercy on us!"

"The young Ship of State" with pennons of victory at the mast-head, and proud banners flung to the breeze, now rode triumphantly upon the tide of popular favor. Souls, that had looked with fear and trembling upon the headlong, impetuous crew, which thronged her decks, no longer doubting, with loud acclaim crowd her sides.

The launch was simply magnificent; the dangerous reef passed safely over, the helmsman, with calm, majestic mien turns to the joy-kindled throng, which press around, and in tones which constrain belief, says: —

"The goal is won! Fear not the ship, my boys. She carries Cæsar!"

Days wore on. Newspapers teemed with glorious

achievements and wonderful valor displayed by brigades, regiments, companies, and individuals: there also was the sickening detail of dead and wounded.

From the Chief Magistrate had come — " our loss is heavy ; " the mourners at home believed it, although the crowds upon the street swore it was nothing, a mere drop in the bucket, compared to Yankee slaughter.

And in fulness of time it was known also that Washington was not taken, nor New York threatened ; and more ; — the smoke of the fagots which were piled high for the base deserters, once Virginia's proud boast, refused to ascend, though expectant hearts called loudly for the torch to be applied.

England and France heard of the unprecedented success of Southern arms, and of the overwhelming defeat of the Army of the Potomac. Still, no tidings of the recognition of the " Young League " by those mighty nations, came to the hearts, which with terrible earnestness watched for them. Consequently the most credulous dropped the voice, and lifted not the foot so high ; and a moderation of self-assurance finally settled down into something like despondency.

CHAPTER XXIII.

VISITORS TO THE MINERAL SPRINGS.

ONCE more the streets were thronged with volunteers, and wealth was lavishly poured into a depleted treasury; while earnest women plied the needle and robbed homes of needful comforts for those whose work was not yet done.

Places of fashionable resort were for the most part abandoned; and sea-breezes and all the allurements of the visiting season forgotten; for a stern and inexorable duty was upon men and women.

The sick could not work, so waters of healing must be resorted to; and officers from the Gulf States also sought for their families a home, where a short furlough from the field of action could be enlivened by the presence of heart-idols.

The "Home," * situated amid the hills of Western North Carolina, celebrated alike for the medicinal properties of its Springs, and the beauty of its scenery, and as its site commanded direct communication with Richmond, which was but twelve hours ride, was doomed to a most uncomfortable notoriety. Most propitiously the season of 1861 opened for the proprietors, but distressingly incommodious for the many, who, wasted by disease, toiled there.

* The Kitrell Spring, N. C.

Amid its crowded halls and spacious parlors we wend our way, and, with unqualified pleasure, feed our eyes upon a few superlatively beautiful representatives from the Gulf States. Haughty, but of exquisite mould, these black-eyed beauties fascinate, dazzle, and bewilder; rich in all the world calls wealth, their every look and movement command the homage of the eye, but not of the heart. By the side of the Mississippi belle, Tennessee, Georgia, and even North Carolina's daughters suffer no disparagement, because less imperious. Comet like, these beautiful beings flash upon us, then are lost amid the crowd of matronly women, invalids, and boisterous children.

And gentlemen were not a few; judges, lawyers, and planters, too old for active service, having given their sons and wealth for liberty, sat down in the pleasant "Home," to greet the coming of the day, whose dawn was kindling the Southern sky. Bachelors gay, and those too crabbed and crotchety, whose want of a wife was, for the first time, keenly felt, (should master and overseer be called into the field without a head, those "held to labor" might enact a scene, detrimental, at least, to the master's interest,) gathered there. The young and pretty passed them by with a sneer; elderly maidens alone laughed gently, as the shuffling gait and wheezy breath announced the approach of lovers

> "At least, well-grown,
> Who used lavender water and eau de cologne."

With night and dancing, officers came from camp near. Of them little can be said, as not merit, but political influence and the ability to raise recruits, was the standard by which rank was distributed.

With the greater part of the gentler sex, industry marks the hour. Earnestly old and young lend themselves to the cutting and making of garments, and the lighter work of knitting, for the destitute sick, who, in canvass tents, within sight of the " Home," are dying by scores. Hands soft and white and sparkling with jewels draw the coarse thread, or wind the cotton, laboriously turn the slow needles.

"See my sock, mamma! all that done, (the *all* consisted of an inch and a quarter of very hubbly knitting,) and but just one week about it!"

The needles are twisted firmly together, the huge ball is stuck on, and the blooming belle, with a sigh of relief that the task for the day — three needles and a half — is over, calls for her hat and cup for the morning's walk to the Spring. The pink on her cheek deepens; is it the consciousness of an effort made to aid her barefooted countrymen which thrills her heart and kindles blushes? Ah, no! From the lofty window her eye catches the dashing approach of officers, imposing with gold lace and gay plumes, and splendidly mounted upon richly caparisoned steeds. Now the call for maids is stunning. With the speed of blackbirds at the crack of the hunter's rifle, small black forms skim the lofty staircases, and return with gloves, gossamer veils, and the jauntiest hats imaginable; a little out of style, but *n'importe*, no New Yorker was there to criticize.

Hasty words bring hasty acts; and hasty acts hasty blows. The ribbon is tied too tight, and the panting maid measures her length upon the floor;

while "You nigger, you pinch me again, and you shall have the lash!" cries the enraged mistress.

"Oh! pray, missis!" the glove is torn; too much haste again; and the torture which the young mulatto suffers, proves conclusively, that the small, delicate fingers which could not knit could pinch — prodigiously!

Hats and gloves are donned at last; and now down the lawn, on through the beautiful grove, creatures of beauty and soldierly mien stroll; the musical fall of water, blending with martial strains, which sweep down from the camps, scattering every despairing sense of the horrors of war, which, with funereal gloom, is settling over their young heads; a war which is to scar the hearts of the survivors with life-long misery.

Proudly boastful of future halcyon days, breathing in the charming aroma of the laurel-leaf crown, Fame's glowing hand holds temptingly near — *you*, who, in soldier garb, tell of a field where imperishable glory is to be won — dream on! Pitying heaven curtains from sight the ghastly horrors of the battle-field, where, smeared with thy own blood, stiffening and clammy with the dews of death, — God calleth!

CHAPTER XXIV.

THE DEATH AND BURIAL OF AN OFFICER.

It was night, but no sound of revelry came from the brilliantly lighted ball-room. A holy hush pervaded the entire house, while grief and weariness were legible on the faces of old and young, who, seated in groups, talked of the solemnity of a soldier's burial that day witnessed.

An officer, on his way to the ball, given at the "Home" on the previous night, had been thrown from his horse and killed instantly. A favorite with his men, and no less popular with the ladies, his death was deeply deplored in camp and parlor. Report said, his father was a Union man, and disowned his son when he took up arms against the Federal Government. Be that as it may, the deceased had exacted the promise from a brother officer, that, if he should survive him, his body should be buried where he fell, and his sword, his only love, laid by his side.

"To think," exclaimed a young lady to her brother, who had just arrived, then on his way to Virginia to join his regiment, "of any man being so inhuman as to deny this young soldier a grave; giving an excuse, that niggers could not be made to work on land where dead men lay. The planter was away at the time the grave was dug, but returned just before the burial, and stubbornly refused to permit the interment. When we arrived at the camp, we heard of this monstrous meanness, and that a spot had been found nearly three miles distant, where the body could be laid.

"Did you ladies follow in the procession that distance, in such a broiling heat as we have experienced to-day?"

"Certainly," chorused the group, to whom the question was addressed.

"But with no very charitable feelings, I assure you, said a Wilmington Miss. "Every sentiment of grief and respect for the dead was swallowed up in wrath, as we toiled through the almost interminable cotton-patch, and over the low ground to the limit of that execrable creature's land. I would stake my fortune, that the man has Yankee blood in him. But here is Mrs. Davis,* approaching; she has lived North, and knows more of the Yankees, than the rest of us. See if she does n't say such a piece of barbarity is on par with all their actions."

"Not so, my young friends," the lady addressed, replied. "There are bad men to be found everywhere: the North, comparatively speaking, has no more than the South.

"But all Northerners are fanatics," persisted the young lady.

"Many of our people entertain the idea that they are, but it is an erroneous one," was the reply. "There is a party North, made up of men, scrupulously observant of the rights granted us by the Con-

---

* Mrs. Jeff. Davis.

stitution; they are at present, impotent to aid us, but their determined resistance to, and abhorrence of the outrages of those, who to gain their infamous ends would trample under foot every human and divine law, we hope will ultimately succeed in checking the frenzy of the hour."

"I see by the faces of these young ladies, my dear madam," said Judge Green, joining the group, "that there is a bitter even in the sweetness, which your lips distil. May I ask, what your remark was, which has banished smiles and caused this brilliant parterre of blooms to droop their delicate heads?"

Before the now smiling lady could reply, she was called away by a servant.

"Papa," said a curly-headed girl, springing to his side, and placing her plump hand in his, "the lady says there are some good men North, and that is what makes us all look so sober."

"Good men North, my little daughter! You certainly misunderstood her."

"But she did, Judge; and although I have all proper respect for Mrs. Davis's opinion, I cannot think but in this assertion she is egregiously mistaken."

"Then I see all my young friends, here, believe with me in the total depravity of the North."

"We do, we do!" chorused a dozen voices. "And instead of whipping us into submission, we have thrashed *them* all soundly, and sent them to beds of torture and repentance."

"Yes, yes," laughed the group.

"God, in signal mercy shown us, has spared the 'Old North State' the foulness the Yankees have heaped upon the once honored cities and towns of Maryland and Virginia," said Francis Bierce, who with his wife had been attracted to the spot by the merriment Judge Green's words aroused.

"Judge," says another of the group, "have you no faith in the report, that the sound we hear from Northern shores, is no death-rattle, but rather the premonitory signal of a deadly spring?"

"Faith, no Captain. It's folly, consummate folly, to waste a thought upon such twattle. I tell you we are done with the Yankees, now and forever!"

"I can't agree with you, Judge, knowing the vindictiveness, the stick-to-a-tive-ness of the Yankees. I know, I feel it too, that before our liberty is achieved, there must be, not a battle, — but battles?"

"Nonsense, Captain, you talk like a child! I tell you the Grand Army of the Potomac is wholly demoralized; the energies of the North completely paralyzed. (More vehemently,) — Don't talk to me about the commotion going on among the Yankees; I tell you sprawling children always holler."

"Ah! Judge," was the rejoinder, "you know no more of the North as a people, than I of the Hottentots. Live with them as I have, then you will believe, as I, that not one blow, nor two, nor a score, such as we gave them at Bull Run, will make them cry "enough." I know no better illustration of their dogged obstinacy, than the habits of the Arctic puffin, which naturalists tell us, when once it has grasped a thing will suffer being drawn from its hole, its limbs torn from its body, and every torture which can be practised upon it, but *never let go*; death only releases the coveted prize. It is just so with the Yankees. Before the pangs of death-telling blows have subsided, lo! four men will take the place of the one shot down, and billions will be held out, with eager hands, where millions were proffered."

"What good did Darius' wealth, and countless numbers do him, Captain Selden?" said a weakly voice. "We are but a handful compared to the North, but *omnipotent*, because we have right on our side."

"Right, madam, right! Our friend, Captain Selden, will do his duty in the field, we all know; but say, ladies, would it not be more becoming his rank, if he would lay down his pair of double million magnifying gas microscopes of hextra power, of Sam Weller's patent, and let common sense tinge his prognostics?"

"I will, I will!" laughed the jolly Captain. "But first promise me, you will buckle on the sword, if a nest of the vermin should be blown to our shores."

"Judge Green," said a lady on his right, tapping his hand with her delicate fan, "papa thinks as Captain Selden, that the worst of the fighting is to come. He says, every man in the South will be in the field before we gain our freedom."

"Who is that young lady?" whispered the evening traveller to his sister, directing her attention to the speaker.

"General Hill's daughter; the General's word is of course recognized authority; but if I were Miss Hill, I would keep such sentiments to myself; they certainly impair her popularity here."

"But ought not. I like her; she is honest and outspoken," was the reply.

"My dear Miss Hill," said the Judge, "no one has a more exalted opinion of your father's ability as

15*

a general, and his devotedness to our cause, than myself. Consider it, therefore, no disparagement upon his great and acknowledged generalship, when I add, we cannot take every word which he utters as oracles;" and then to Captain Selden, — "Well, if we admit that our present force may be called into the field and cut to pieces, we have a reserve, which cannot be conquered. Two millions of slaves, *armed*, would be invincible, whatever the opposing force."

"Such a reserve can never be brought into the field! never, Judge, never!"

"It can! I maintain it can! I myself have four hundred negroes," said the Judge, rising and laying his hand forcibly upon the captain's shoulder, "and what is more," he continued, with increasing vehemence, "there is not one of them but would stand by me, while there was a drop of blood in my veins, and fight like demons over my dead body!"

"I haven't a quarter of that number, Judge Green, and I am called an easy master; now I speak what I know, when I say not one of my negroes, but would make good his escape, should the way be open to the North."

The disputants had gradually withdrawn from the group of ladies, and as the debate waxed warmer, a crowd began to collect; and, what was noticeable, the Captain, who with one frail girl, stoutly persisted in the peril of the hour, and openly rebuked the exaggerated self-confidence of his associates, was heavily reinforced, when the practicability of arming the negroes was discussed, by stout hearts, that spurned the slave unarmed, but feared him as a famished tiger, when cold iron gave him the power of self-assertion.

CHAPTER XXV.

NEWS FROM WASHINGTON.

"OH! the torment of little things! Hateful Yankees!" cries the beautiful pianist, as she pulls up the key which would not sound; "no piano, no music, nothing! all for you!"

From lips white with anger the goblet is dashed, and the water (uniced) is splashed upon the marble slab.

Pianos, purchased to replace cracked kettle-drums, went *back* instead of into Southern ports. Ice (and what is life South without ice) had been shipped for Southern markets; so had medicine, for the want of which chills and fever, bilious and typhoid, raged unmitigated; but Abe Lincoln's ships, bristling with guns and manned by desperate men, stopped the way.

Therefore, tepid water must be drunk; and the eye followed the flow of butter in amber streams from pitchers. Songs rose loud and clear, but no efforts of the gifted songstress could drown the discordant accompaniment, which carried one back to the haunted chambers of youth's distempered fancy. For want of strings, harps and guitars' lay by, unswept; and oh, sad, sad words! fever patients and ague subjects, racked with pain, then pale and languishing, dreamed of quinine and soothing cordials, and woke to curse the light which tortured them, the darkness which strengthened their pangs, to curse the North and die.

The piano has stopped. Music, talking, and even heart-burnings are stayed, for the *Evening Post*, just brought in, teems with good news.

"Overtures of peace from Washington!" shouts the portly Judge Green, bouncing from his chair; "I told you so; all right, Captain ——; to dictate our own terms, too. Ha! ha! ha! Dixie has blown up a storm which has capsized Uncle Sam's old craft! See the old hull! she's unshipped her helm, her sails are torn, her seams open to the engulphing waves. Hark! here's a signal gun of distress! Let the rotten old craft go down amid the breakers which have stove her; and woe to the man, woman, or child that throws a rope or a spar, to save the drowning wretches!"

Amen! was the hearty response.

The excited man read extract after extract from the *New York Herald*, and here's another "hear, hear," and the no less excited crowd cheer and clap, then listen in breathless silence, and then cheer again for Dixie, as extracts from Northern papers fill their eager ears.

The demonstrations of exultant delight, which followed the reading of the "papers," whose verity few doubted, have, in a measure, subsided, and now, singly or in groups, the visitors at the "Home" lend themselves to the coveted papers which bear the long-expected tidings, "Peace sueing," the recognition of the "Southern Confederacy."

When Judge Green, to the astonishment of every one, read from a Southern paper, — the *Post*, — while great drops of sweat stand out, bead-like, upon his flushed face, (a very safe channel for the exuberance of such joy to vent itself,) the programme to a new play which has just been brought out, at ——, called, " Picayune Butler, is coming out to-night, Crowded houses, Tremendous excitement ! " &c. &c.

" You all know Picayune Butler," cries the Judge, " the meanest of all men, — ladies, your presence forbids my expressing a more emphatic opinion of the ' Knave.' "

" The programme reads, 1st part — Picayune Butler is represented in league with the ' Devil and imps,' for the possession of ' Booty and Beauty,' of a fair Southern city. A contract is drawn up, by which Butler receives the services of his horned compeer. Butler plans, the cloven-foot gently executes.

" Part 2d — The barricades of the city are shaken as if by an earthquake. Butler looks on and smiles, (as the way is cleared for him to march in and take possession,) ' It is mine,' cries the mad man, as his eyes gloat over the beauty and gold the doomed city discloses. ' Not so,' cries the ' Prince of darkness ; ' ' one such soul as thine I must have. So reads the compact : I have gone from ocean to ocean, from heights of the mountains to the lowest depth of the valleys, yet I have not found one such as thee.' ' Did'st find none at Wheatland ? ' gasped Butler, writhing with torture as the gripe which held him tightened upon his flesh. ' And shall I buy what is mine own ? Not so reads the compact. Go *thou*, and seek a soul like thine ; I'll hold the city.'

" Part 3d — Butler goes and returns, and goes

again. 'Not such as *thine*,' was the stern reply, while weary and worn with much watching, 'goin' to and fro the earth,' the *watchman* sleepeth, but awakes to find himself shorn of his tail, horns, and cloven-foot, which the wily Butler had appropriated. 'Die!' cries the new beast, as he bends over him; 'thou my master? earth nor hell has no match for thee,' cries the defenceless compeer. The keys of the bottomless pit and thy life is spared,' says his master.

"Part 4th — Then follows the descent of the 'Great new beast' into the infernal regions, there to bind his servant, and whom else he pleases, while *he* ravishes the earth.

"Part 5th — The curtain rises, for the last time, upon a man loathsome and haggard, hideous to look upon, chained to an iron staple in his cell. 'I have dreamed!' he cries, shaking his manacled hands; 'aye! dreamed that earth and hell were mine; that such as I earth would not bind, nor hell restrain. But Dixie! Dixie! Dixie!' in agonizing tones, came from those dying lips; 'What heaven nor hell could do, thou hast done!' Under the door, bread and water! and the mad man, frensied with want, clanked his chains, and, in paroxysms of rage, bites his flesh. 'Booty and Beauty,' laughs the jailer at the grated window, while the sparkling glass and wheaten loaf are lifted high. The glaring eyeballs and gibbering lips devours the sight. 'Give! give!' and skeleton hands claw the air. 'Booty and Beauty' rings through the lowest depths of 'Castle Thunder!' The glass and bread left in tempting sight, the jailer flown. As Death draws near, Reason kindles the glassy eye. It turns from the fearful wreck, the fleshless bones, to the breast in the grated window. The trembling lips unclose — ' Woman, thou art avenged!' A groan, a shudder, and the lifeless form falls to the earth."

A burst of overwhelming applause followed the reading of the programme.

"To die and be eaten of worms, is too mild a death for such a monster. Let him set foot on the soil of my honored State, and tortures, and death that he dreams not of, await him."

"Well spoken for you, Bierce," said a voice from the crowd. But if he should light upon us some day, what would you do?"

"Take him prisoner, of course; then hand him over to the ladies to dispose of."

"But, my dear husband," said Mrs. Bierce, "you know I should not let you go out to meet such a piece of abomination; you meant you would detail your niggies to do the vile work."

"Of course, wife, I am but joking; the infamous Butler is dead, without question."

"Hear! Hear!" cries Judge Green; "I am chosen chairman of the committee of arrangements to take the young ladies, to-morrow night, to witness the grand play of 'Picayune Butler coming out to-night.' What gentlemen offer their services?"

The list, soon swelled to some length, was read by Capt. Selden, very deliberately, and then handed back to Miss Green.

"Your name, of course, I shall put down?"

"Not so, madam."

"You surely will not deny us the pleasure of your company?"

"I have not the slightest desire to see this *sham Butler.*"

"It will be a pleasing relaxation from camp duty."

"I find all I need here."

"Ridiculous! Captain, say you will go; see, I have your name down; and don't plead camp duties an excuse for not seeing the Yankee Butler give up the ghost."

"If you please, strike off my name from your list, my young friend, and put it on the roll where Ben Butler, if he lives, is to be found. I would like to meet him face to face in the field."

"What! meet that execrable monster?"

"Meet him? yes; if he is the coward report says he is, he is mine; if a soldier, and better armed than myself, I may be his."

"Don't speak of it; I should shudder at the very thought of such an encounter, if I did not know that the vile creature was dead, and buried out of sight."

"How do you know that?"

"Not seeing his name paraded before the public is proof infallible that the Yankees have permitted one of their gods to sleep."

"If that is the case, I see no cause in heaping such imprecations on Ben Butler; he is the least of all the rascals that has brought this trouble upon us; look to the masters, not to the monkey and dogs, that have been taught bloody theft, if you would put a stop to such depredations."

"Do, mamma, come here," said the fair pleader to an elderly lady who was passing; "Captain Selden refuses to go to —to-morrow, to witness the great play. I must go on with my list; will leave him in your hands, and do you mould him to my will."

"I am glad to hold some conversation with you, Captain."

"Speak on, madam."

"I have unbounded confidence in your judgment."

"Yes, madam, but what would you say?" Taking the proffered chair, his interlocutor resumed: "I am much disheartened to know, if the terms of peace offered by the Yankees, and accepted at Richmond, will compel us to resign all hopes of possessing New York? You must know,"— with true invalid look and voice she continued, — "that I have been in the habit of going to Saratoga yearly, and, in my present infirm state of health, Congress water is indispensable. It is, however, quite out of the question for me to think of going to Saratoga, Newport, or any other place North, until we have possession of two or three of the Yankee States at least. Now, what I want to know of you, is, how soon we may claim, say, Pennsylvania and New York, as our own?"

"Never! madam," was the emphatic reply.

"Never?" gasped suffering secesh; "why, what do you mean by that?"

"I mean, that those who would visit Northern cities, must do so under Northern auspices."

"You misunderstand me, Captain. Not one of us dream of going North, until we can call this place and that, our own. I am speaking now of a treaty of peace between our people and the North. In what way shall we be benefited, if we consent to negotiate with them?"

"What treaty of peace have you reference to?"

"Why, you heard Judge Green read, a short time since, of a committee having been sent from Washington to Richmond, with propositions looking to the restoration of peace."

"That was a fabrication."

"What was a fabrication?"

"What the Judge read."

"Captain, it is a very grave charge to bring against any of our papers, — this fabricating stories to tickle the public ear! We may look for wholesale falsehood among Yankee people, where lying is an indigenous talent, but —"

"Madam," said the Captain, interrupting, "the *Post*, which Judge Green read from, is a sensation paper, and no sensible person would waste a thought on the matter contained in it."

"What paper then contains reliable news?" very despondingly was asked.

"The *Richmond Examiner* is, in my estimation, the only paper worth the reading."

"O dear! O dear! If what you say be true, and our papers *are* up to lying, we can't expect to be prospered. But do tell me, Captain, if the North does not offer to make peace, what we may expect next?"

"A fight, more sanguinary even than the last."

"Then I hope Beauregard will be allowed to push on North, as he wished to do after the Bull Run affair. I am convinced, that if Joe Johnson had been out of the way, and Beauregard had been allowed to carry out his plans, I should now be sipping my Congress water with the dignified grace of one, who is monarch of all she surveys."

"That was the first and last chance that Dixie had for Northern conquest," was the rejoinder. "Some one of our generals has said, 'we delayed to march upon Washington in the critical moment of destiny, and having neglected to do so, the tide of fortune is turned against us. Now, we shall do well to hold our own!' He was right, and I believe it, from my heart."

"But, Captain, if, with all the fight, which is in our soldiers, we can't hold our own and gain what is absolutely essential to our comfort, let a draft be resorted to."

"One thing we must have, and that is New York city, before Christmas, draft or no draft," said a merry voice at the Captain's elbow.

"You here, Miss Mary?" he said, turning; "I thought the dance possessed irresistible charms for you."

"So it does, usually, but yours and mamma's earnest faces attracted me here; say now, think you I am too sanguine of spending a merry Christmas in the Empire State?"

"First, tell me how we shall obtain possession of that much coveted State?"

"By assault, of course."

"How shall such assault be made, by land, or water?"

"Now, Captain, you are laughing at me. You know, as well as I, we shall approach New York by Washington."

"Washington is ours, then?"

"You know it soon will be."

"No, my young friend, I know no such thing. I was saying to your mother, as you approached, we shall do well to hold our own."

"Hold our own, indeed! Of course we shall do that, and take what we want from our thievish neighbors, also. Every one says you are a brave man, Captain Selden," she added, with an arch smile; "the wonder is, you use such weak words."

"Better a weak tongue, than a stomach that can digest only sugar-plums."

"And you class *me* among that weakly sort of people?"

"Yes, Miss Mary, and worse," said the blunt Captain. "I call all men and women cowards, who say the Yankee is yet to be born, who can turn them one foot from his track; and I regret to add, not a lady of my acquaintance here, but has avowed the same. As for the men, they have perjured themselves fearfully, if 'back to the foe' is written against them."

"And do *you* advocate Yankee skedaddling?"

"I recommend discretion in all things. Were I overpowered, and saw a chance to save my life by taking to my heels, I am quite sure I should make the attempt; and I am almost as sure, should the Yankees approach your city and threaten to shell it, not one of you ladies but would seek an asylum in our Western hills."

"*I*, never! I would brave danger and death even in defence of my beautiful home; were we in Baltimore, I could convince you my courage is not of words."

"Washington may have its turn as well as Baltimore."

A merry laugh followed the Captain's suggestion.

"Why not, Miss Mary?"

"For the very stubborn fact, that it will keep the Yankees sleepless to defend their own Washington; our troops are now at its very gates!"

"We must not forget the North has a navy. Think you they will allow their ships to rot in their harbors, when the cry for cotton is so urgent?"

"But the world can't have Southern cotton until Abe Lincoln is made to raise the blockade."

"*That* is for the strongest party to maintain."

"If we find we are to be overpowered, we can burn our cotton, and refuse to plant more."

"Then we burn our own fingers."

"I question that."

"We all say 'cotton is king.' Now, if we are mad enough to burn what, at present, alone constitutes our wealth, to prevent its falling into Yankee hands, and refuse to plant more, we throw away the only key which unlocks us to the world."

A commotion was at this moment heard in the outer hall; and a brother officer, with marked agitation approaching, whispered to the Captain, and the two hurriedly left the room.

CHAPTER XXVI.

BUTLER PANIC.

MORNING broke over the "Home" in showers of golden light. Nature looked up and smiled, but perjured man, maddened at the retributive justice his crime had called down on his own head, — cursed.

With dawn, vociferous heralds came from the camps with —

"Forts Hatteras and Clark have fallen! Butler leads the Vandals!"

The dreamers of yesterday — where are they? In chambers, parlor, and halls, stern men d — m the Yankees with faint breath: women, pale with fright, toss their hands in wild despair, and call piteously upon husbands, brothers, and sons. *Where are they?*

Conquered, humiliated, they lie huddled in proud ships, canopied by the colors they have failed to strike, and stung to the soul by the martial strains, which led on their ancestors to valorous deeds and imperishable renown.

The panic-stricken visitors at the "Home" watch shudderingly for the morning mail; it comes, and their worst fears are confirmed.

"Read!" shouts the frantic crowd. From a strong voice on the right —

"Forts Hatteras and Clark have fallen! The key to Albemarle Sound is in the hands of Northern Vandals! Yankee gunboats, filled with brutal invaders, infest the Neuse, the Tar, and Roanoke! Washington, Newbern, and Beaufort are at the mercy of the foe!" Then followed the particulars of the engagement, "which was heroically sustained by a mere handful of men against an overwhelming force of Yankees, the carnage on the decks of the Yankee squadron telling the accurate aim of Carolina's brave boys."

From a gathering on the left, we hear: —

"The forts could have held out until reinforcements arrived from Newbern, had they not been basely betrayed by a traitor, who signalled to the fleet, where the only landing could be effected.

* * * * *

"Commodore Barron, the traitor, was seen shaking hands with Brute Butler on the ship's deck!"

* * * * *

"A greater calamity could not have befallen us. The coast of Virginia, from Norfolk to Cape Lookout, is at the mercy of Yankee gunboats! The peril which threatens is appalling! To arms! men, women, and children! Brickbats are at hand, when guns and powder fail! To the shores! The guns of the iron monsters already rend the air! The yells of the invaders pierce our ears!"

The scene at the "Home" is one of direful confusion. Hurrying of feet, packing of trunks, calls for coach, buggy, hack, and wagon, a sob and an oath, a cry for help, and tearful farewells, fill the air;

while poopoohing at " cowards constitutionally " drops into the deep bass of unmitigated wrath:

"In holy anger and pious grief,
 They solemnly cursed the rascally thieves;
 They cursed them at board, they cursed them in bed,
 From the sole of the foot to the crown of the head.
 They cursed them in sleeping, that every night
 They should dream of the devil, and wake in a fright;
 They cursed them in eating, they cursed them drinking,
 They cursed them in laughing, in sneezing, in winking,
 They cursed them in walking, in riding, in fleeing;
 They cursed them living, they cursed them dying;
 Never was heard such a terrible cursing!"

And oh! the flight of those panic-stricken ones. Some to the gates of the beleagured cities for home treasures, but by far the greater number, in mad haste, sought the fastnesses of the Blue Ridge, where the sullen jar of cannon and the fall of cities might not come.

"From morn till eve the sad array
 Urged on its melancholy way;
 Women and children swelled the tide,
 And old age tottered by their side."

With home-bound ones we push on; yet not far, for armed men fill the cars. A carriage is secured, but still, many miles from loved ones, we find our course impeded by faint and weary pilgrims who block the road.

"[Nabob and negro] side by side,
 Commingling in one motley tide."

CHAPTER XXVII.

MAGGIE AND RALPH.

COME with me, reader, among *other* actors on the world's wide stage, upon whom the 28th of August rose cloudless. Before the finger upon the dial of time marked the day far spent, wondering eyes were turned to the heavens. Quick, sharp thunder-claps heralded a storm, but still no cloud obscured the blue expanse above; clap succeeded clap, yet no storm-cloud, no flash.

"Somebody is getting it," says the merchant, as he complacently rubs his hands. "The storm will not trouble us," and he turns from the lookout to the cool counting-room.

"There's a storm brewing," growls the sportsman, and he shoulders his gun and whistles to his hounds.

"Mighty big thunder," chuckles Sambo, in the corn-field; and he too scans the heavens for the rain-cloud which will send niggers to cover.

But before night a sound was heard, which shook homes and terror-smitten hearts, as if an earthquake spoke. *That sound*—"The Yankees are on us! Yankee gunboats boom along our shores!"

Maggie Blout, a prisoner in her own house, with a heart tortured by the uncertainty of the fate of one she had risked her life to save (who had been betrayed into the hunter's power), and by the absence of her Cousin Harry, whom the world called dead, — a word had reached her that he was well, and would soon strike home for her, — endured the days of her captivity with that self-sustaining energy which defies calamities, beneath the weight of which weaker minds would sink.

Frigidly affable, Ralph Bierce met his captive daily at the board; there he carelessly recounted the events of the hour; for all intercourse with the world without, and all newspapers, had been interdicted from the moment Ralph's hand had fallen upon her trust.

"Those are Yankee guns, Cousin Margaret," he said, as he sought her side that August morning. "I will thread your needle; those trembling hands can never do it."

As Maggie quietly declined his assistance, he added —

"Why so moved? you have nothing to fear."

"Fear! Ralph, conscience only makes cowards."

"You are very white, and I see your breath comes hurriedly; nay, do not struggle to conceal your emotion, for I can assure you the Yankees can neither harm me nor aid you."

"Your welfare does not particularly interest me, nor am I so selfish as to think of myself, when brave men are falling like autumn leaves, perhaps at each blast of those distant guns."

"Were you to die to-morrow, and a violent death might be averted by those same Yankees pegging away at our forts, this booming of cannon —"

"Ralph, speak out; what do you insinuate?"

"What, by your looks, I know you divine."

"Why torture me so?"

"Would it ease your heart to know, that to-morrow Richard Wheddon dies?"

"If he must die," and Maggie spoke slowly and firmly, "better it should be so, than to drag out a miserable existence in a loathsome cell."

"Such resignation is truly sublime! I thought it woman's nature to weep, when robbed of heart's idols; but you, Margaret, do sit here unmoved, as the rope swings, which is to launch a sin-smitten soul into eternity. What a commentary upon the faithlessness of woman's love!"

"That I do, Ralph, and smile too, but not at the approaching death of a man, the daily beauty of whose life makes yours hateful; I smile at the mean malignity that his unswerving fidelity to his country has aroused; for I know, and you know also, that, deadly as your enmity is towards him, not one hair of the head God has set his seal upon, can you or your minions harm."

"Tell me, Margaret, where the waters of purification are to be found, where befoul traitors and *effétés intriguantes* go down, and come up saints and singing angels? I would dip, and be counted worthy to be numbered with such shining lights," Ralph said in his usual sarcastic tone.

"Your sainted mother taught me where the true waters of comfort are to be found."

"Hold! my mother's name is sacred; speak it not!" and the proud man bowed his head as if smitten by an unseen hand; then, rising, paced the room hurriedly.

Maggie gathered up her work, and rose to leave her cousin's presence. As she laid her hand upon the door-knob, Ralph was by her side. "Stay, and hear what I would say," he said.

Refusing the chair he motioned for her to take, yet grasping his extended hand, Maggie said: —

"Ralph, for your mother's sake, I wish we were friends."

"You speak of my mother. Had she lived, I should not be the man I am, wrecked and ruined by the woman who bears my father's name. Though so young when she died, I loved her with all the fervor of my nature; had she lived, a life's homage would have been too little for the wealth of affection she lavished on me. But she died, and I live to curse heaven —"

"Stop, Ralph; curse the abode where your angelic mother calls you! Learn to love what she loved, and there is an eternity for you to spend together."

"Go! Margaret," and, as he spoke, he dropped her hand; "your woman's tongue unmans me."

She glanced up to the dark face, which was partially turned from her. Grief and contrition were plainly stamped there; and the sight of a tear on his swarthy cheek made her heart bound with inexpressible joy. "Cousin Ralph may be saved yet," she thought. "Love of thee, dear Aunt Mary, is the only 'green blade of joy' in that blasted heart. May thy angelic presence guide the stumbling steps of thy first-born, best-loved child!"

Through the long evening Maggie sat at her window, and, although peals of distant thunder sounded at intervals, she paid no heed; for the execution of the morrow weighed heavily upon her spirits. "O Harry, Harry, why are you not here?" she breathed aloud; "no kindly sympathy, no loving word; dear, dear Harry come back!"

A step upon the walk aroused her. She raised

her head, for her heart whispered, "he has come!" But no, "only Dr. Pill," she sighed. As she leaned from the window, she noted that the man, who was not an infrequent visitor of Ralph, was listening intently, and counting on his fingers the sharp claps which sounded now at shorter intervals. Ralph's words, "Yankee guns," came to her, but she shut her heart, and would not indulge the wild throb of delight, which his words at first excited. Pushing wide the blinds, "I will watch the storm," she thought. "God's voice is in the whirlwind; it may speak peace to my— Great God! and can it be?" burst from her, as her eye swept that quarter of the heavens resonant with thunder-claps where not a cloud, not a miniature float obscured the dazzling brightness of the glowing concave. "God be praised! the *Yankees are here*, on our very coast," and she clapped her hands in ecstasy of joy, as a continuous roar shook the air, and died, and rose anew.

"Amen to that, lady!"

Maggie dropped her eyes, and they rested upon Dr. Pill. Stout, but misshapen, dressed in coarse garments he stood; uncovered as to his head, for his one hand held the felt hat, which a true feeling of chivalry had raised, although he boasted no "descent from English cavaliers."

Quickly she drew back. "There is something about that man which strangely affects me," she murmured; "what can he have to do with Ralph? He must indeed be an arch-dissembler, if a Union man, to dupe my shrewd cousin. I remember now, it was after one of his calls here, I found that word from Harry, pencilled on papa's bust; he may have news for me to-day. There, that was what I read in his face; and he shall bear tidings of Mr. Whedden's imminent danger to Harry."

The few words were written with a trembling hand, and once more, with unwonted cheerfulness, Maggie had seated herself at the window to await the doctor's reappearance, when a summons came to meet Ralph in the parlor.

"Margaret," he said, on meeting her there, "news has just come which calls me to the city. Dr. Pill confirms what I told you this morning. The Yankees are upon our coast, ten to one of the force, which man our forts. Men have been sent for; I leave with the company which goes from our city." Then, dropping his voice, he continued; "Your reputation, your life is in my hands; one word of mine, and the prisoner's doom is yours. The negro who betrayed you is dead; those you have here are devoted to you. I go away, Margaret, but put not out your hand again to rescue these accursed Yankee sympathizers. This time I spare you, for I would hurt no thing my mother smiled upon; but now I warn you, as there is power in law, your life is forfeited, if you raise but a finger again to aid proscribed heads. The woman I sought here has slipped through my fingers. I have to thank *you* for that. I have track of her; you look as if you doubted it, but it is true. No woman outwits me but once; remember that, and remember, also, what awaits you if you set aside my threat."

Without waiting for a reply, Ralph turned away, and, with Dr. Pill, left the house. Hardly had the door closed upon them, when the loved bust was raised. There lay a slip of paper, and Maggie read thereon: —

" Men in our town built a jail,
And a tall man put within it.
Yankee Doodle came to town,
Yankee Doodle dandy;
Nothing in it, nothing in it,
But the bricks around it!"

CHAPTER XXVIII.

RICHARD WHEDDEN'S ESCAPE.

"NEVER!" said an intrepid girl, as the warning, "Run, the Yankees are on us!" reached her; and a smile lit up her face as her eye fell upon the heavily shotted weapons which lay near.

"Run, missis, run! old Butler'll catch you," cried her maid, bustling into the room.

"No, Kizzie, never! I fear no Yankees while I have so good a friend as this; it never fails me," and she laid her hand upon her treasure defiantly.

"Missis is a powerful shot, I knows, and a mighty sight braver than them white folks runnin' yonder. See, see, they come this way!"

Mistress and maid leaned from the window, and a scornful smile played over the watcher's face, as she marked the crowd of young men and maidens, old men and children, who, panic-smitten, rushed pell-mell through the streets to the depot.

"Fly, Miss Bierce, — not a moment to lose! The Yankees are in sight!" Again she uttered that single word, "Never!" and the breathless youth quickened his steps as, with the word, her eye flashed, "coward."

A man in the city's loathsome jail heard the tumult without, and, with a look which spoke a soul at peace, turned to meet the assassins who sought his life. With a blow, the low door flew wide, and a strong man entered.

"Be you Richard Whedden, what was to be hung?" he cried.

"That is my name."

A low chuckle, a whispered word succeeded, and the tall, gaunt man sprung to his feet, and followed his bandy-legged, one-armed guide to the door, where a cart and mule were in waiting. With a powerful lift, the prisoner was safely placed in the cart, and the rude driver, leaping in after him, shouted, as he lashed his mule amid the press of fugitives:

"Split ahead, Dixie!—clear the track, niggers!— jump in write trash! Yankee gun-boats, slam up to the city!" then to his mule, "mind you, Sal, what did I feed you for? Tear ahead, Dixie,—forty miles to Weltown! Thunder and blitzen, we creep like snails!" and the mad driver alternately cheered and mocked the struggling crowd, lashing on his mule the while.

"Forty miles to Weltown!" but with the accompanying fortieth lash, the animal, with a leap, cleared the rope harness, and down went the cart, out shot Jehu, away went mule! Apparently in no way disconcerted by the jeers and threats which assailed him, the prostrate man shouted, "Forty miles to Weltown! hurry up, friends, I'm with you!" Then, on regaining his feet, he deliberately wiped the blood and dirt from his bruised face, and dragged his cart to the shelter of the trees by the roadside.

"Served you right, you cruel man, for beating your mule so unmercifully," Helen said, for the catastrophe had occurred before her window. The man heard the words, and looking up, saw the laughing faces bent down upon him. A bow and grimace followed, and the cap was snatched from the mop of matted hair, to be jammed down upon the head of the man who lay doubled up among the fodder bundles which were in the cart; and, in a twinkling, the quaint driver was lost to sight.

"See! Missis, see!" cried Kizzie, directing her mistress's attention, which had wandered to the crowd, again to the cart and owner.

One look, and Helen sprung to the steps. Too late! for the noble bay was in the ropes. With a bound into the cart, and a low whistle, the bold robber, capless, whipless, without a rein to guide the plunging horse, dropped his body in mocked obeisance to the enraged fair one, while "Forty miles to Weltown! jump in, ma'am; free ride for nothing!" came back on the wind.

"Villain! robber!" but her voice was lost in the rattle of the bounding cart. "I might have shot him," she said, bending forward to see the last of the priceless horse. "Oh, Ralph; Ralph, what will you say!"

"Massa Ralph will roar now!" chuckles Kizzie, from her lookout. "Served him right, though; 't aint his horse, no how; be took him from Miss Maggie's stable 'cause Massa Harry did n't come home from the war."

CHAPTER XXIX.

HEROISM.

On the day following Ralph's departure, Maggie sits quietly at her window, watching the flight of the terror-smitten ones, which the city has poured forth.

"More frightened than hurt," she cries, as her eye caught sight of a low cart, which was whirled furiously on, amid men, women, and children, pack-horse, mule, and shoat. "What a mad animal! is his owner dead with fright, that he does not guide the wild creature?"

When in full view of the house, a capless head shot up from the cart, and a handkerchief held high over it streamed out upon the wind.

"It is Dr. Pill! he surely signals me!" and Maggie leaned from the window to wait for the dust to lift, to catch another glimpse of the fleet runaways. The heavy dust cloud rose at length, but winged steed, cart, driver, and flag had vanished!

The successful flight of Dr. Pill brought vividly to Maggie's mind his rude rhyme; and, in order that you, indulgent reader, may appreciate the absorbing and complete happiness the thought of Mr. Wheddon's probable escape afforded her, and the intense joy which her own freedom inspired, a brief retrospect is necessary; one, which shall place you in possession of the events which followed her house being taken forcible possession of by Ralph Bierce and his armed followers.

News had come, through Dr. Hall, that Mr. Weasel, though dangerously shot by the guard at Salisbury, still lived. Mrs. Weasel's resolution was at once taken; and, under her assumed name, Fay, she bent her untiring energies to the fulfilment of her project, to reach and aid him. The hour had come, which was to see her once more a wanderer; a pilgrim, whose Mecca was the couch of her husband; that husband, a man who would suffer torture, yes, death, but not infamy; who feared to live a traitor, but dared to bless his country and die as only brave men can.

Pomp, who had safely carried the boy, Percy, to the McGowans for protection, had returned from the long day's ride, and now waited at the edge of the wood with his master's fleet horse, for the mother.

"Back 'fore de sun's up, and Massa Ralph know nothin' 'bout dis yer night's work," chuckled the honest soul, as he patted the neck of his horse.

There was no moon, no starlight to guide the travellers; but the keen slave needed none, — "senses always told him when things went wrong." Already had he waited the few moments which Aunt Lizzie said were necessary for final fixings, but there was no sound of approaching steps. Pomp, though the most patient of human beings, grew restless as the minutes grew longer and longer; he walked to the road, from the road to the buggy, and back again, but no footfall, save his own, broke the stillness of the night. He gazed at the house. "Trouble up dar, sartain," he said. Then he remembered if anything occurred to mar their arrangements, a light was to be placed in the hall-window. With a sigh he turned again to his horse, and was patting his soft, silky coat, when a glimmer through the trees lit up the darkness of the woods, and kindled the silver mountings of the pet's gear. In a moment more, Pomp, with flying leaps, was nearing the house.

"You are nervous," said Maggie, as she helped her friend draw on her gloves. "Have no more fear; everything has worked charmingly. Lizzie tells me our jailer has gone to his room, and Pomp waits up the road."

Mrs. Fay, white as the cap, which was drawn snugly about her face, laid her head upon Maggie's shoulder, and, in that tearful embrace, thanked God that, in her, her children and herself had found such a friend.

"No thanks are due me," said Maggie, struggling to subdue her own emotion, "except that, with paint and gray hair, I have made you such a nice-looking grandmamma. Now mind," she added, shaking her finger threateningly, "do not rub your eyes, if car-dust and cinders threaten to put your eyes out; for one brush of your handkerchief would quite efface these perfect wrinkles. Remember, too, to forget to blush, if complimented upon your green old age, for red cheeks and wrinkles are at variance; and, lastly, cough violently if questioned, for you cannot disguise your voice; but, beyond Raleigh, you are safe. Then toss cap, paint, and cough to the winds. There are other changes of dress packed in the valise; in them you will be so completely disguised, no one but your own dear husband will recognize you."

"I doubt much if he would recognize me even in

my own garb, for I feel I have changed sadly since we were parted."

"You have lost nothing but what his presence will restore, I am confident. But hark! there is Lizzie at the door." Maggie drew the bolt; "Softly, Lizzie, softly," she whispered, "Ralph is a light sleeper."

"But wakes, Margaret, to counterplot!"

The unlooked-for appearance of her cousin made the brave girl quail for a moment; but, regaining her composure, and holding the door-knob in her hand, she said: "May I ask what occasions this intrusion at so unreasonable an hour?"

"I would see the lady who shares your private apartment," he made answer, pushing the door rudely open, and entering the room.

At the sound of his voice, with instinctive quickness, Mrs. Fay had shut off the gas, but had unconsciously dropped the valise. Over it the intruder tripped, and fell heavily upon the floor; and, before he had regained his feet, the door was closed and locked behind the retreating figures of Maggie and her friend. "What have we done?" cried Mrs. Fay, quickly checking the smothered laughter, the thought of the fouler trapped had aroused.

"Done! why turned the tables handsomely upon my gentlemanly cousin, and made him my captive, until he promises more decorous deportment!" and a merry, ringing laugh followed Maggie's words.

"But Mr. Whedden! he is in the adjoining room; his light will attract your cousin's notice."

Thought of the danger which threatened Mr. Whedden at first seemed to paralyze Maggie; but, shortly regaining in some degree her stricken faculties, she sprung to the bell-rope, and pulled it violently. As no servant appeared to her repeated summons, she coolly and deliberately turned to her companion, saying; "I see it all now. Ralph thought to have his own way; to cut me off from aid, and then compel me to have my room searched. I must think for a moment, and then act."

Maggie possessed a quick, comprehensive mind, — one which could easily and effectively call into play whatever resources the emergency of a case might find within reach; and now, when such fearful peril threatened her friends and herself, her powers of perception seemed doubly quickened, and the project conceived found her with ready means for its execution.

"Mrs. Fay," she said, "you must not delay your departure longer than is absolutely necessary. I know Ralph would not undertake to use force here without assistance. As he has disposed of my servants, I must myself reconnoitre; if I find the way clear to the road, you must run to the woods. Pomp will soon be here; if anything should prevent his return, you must drive yourself to Weltown. But stay here," she added, throwing open the library door, "I shall make but a short delay."

The light in the hall-window being placed as a signal for Pomp, the intrepid mistress commenced her search about the grounds; and not ten minutes had elapsed ere she had regained her friend's side.

"There are two men on the lawn, on the watch, probably," she said; "and, although they are white men, Pomp and I are a match for them."

"There may be even more; what can you and Pomp do if it should prove so?"

"Fight!" and the word came strong and clear.

"Maggie, I cannot go, and leave you in such peril."

"But you must, Mrs. Fay," Maggie said, resolutely; and, firmly but kindly checking further entreaties, she gave her full directions to gain the road by way of the garden. "With no horse but Harry's would I trust you. Nise knows the way; give her the reins, and she will carry you swiftly and safely. When in Weltown, cut her loose; she will find her way back. Here is gold," she added, thrusting a heavy purse into her hand; "buy what you will need in Raleigh, but for your life do not stop before reaching there."

One short embrace, and the friends parted. Overshadowed by the wings of Mercy, her feet bound with Faith's golden sandals, which made rough places smooth, and lighted up the valley of distrust and foreboding, the fearless mother stepped boldly into peril's track, and challenged the foe. Here for the present we must leave her, for our narrative leads us to Maggie and her household.

"Ralph has deprived me of my servants; now he shall try a hand at fighting his battles alone," she said, as, having secured the outer doors, she turned to a richly-inlaid cabinet, and drew therefrom three heavy pistol-cases. The pistols were ready cocked, and, putting one into her belt, and grasping the other determinately, she walked calmly to her chamber door. As she passed the window, she heard heavy steps upon the walk. "Pomp!" "Yes, missis." "To the west veranda!" she cries.

He is safely in, and the door made fast behind him. Of him, Maggie learns that two men and a negro were on his steps; that he saw their faces distinctly by the hall light, but escaped them by dodging under the east veranda, and creeping under the house to the west front.

"Go to the hall, Pomp; take the pistol I have laid there for you; then follow me. We will avoid bloodshed if possible, but one thing is sure; Mr. Whedden must be saved at any cost."

Maggie and her powerful ally mounted the broad staircase, and, at the door of that front room, they stopped.

"Stand here, Pomp! let no one pass except Mr. Whedden; if Ralph attempts it, and threatens force, fire, but not without; we must keep him here, until Mr. Whedden has made good his escape to the garden." As she spoke, she drew from her pocket a key, and, fitting it to the lock, turned it and entered the chamber. The room was well lighted, and in an arm-chair, in a manner indicative of perfect repose, Ralph Bierce reclined, reading the evening paper.

He glanced carelessly up to the pale, determined face which met his look, and, as his eye fell upon the weapon she held in her hand, and upon the other in her girdle, he smiled ironically, and resumed his reading.

The half-open door of the adjoining room caught Maggie's attention. She advanced, and threw it wide open. The gas was burning, but the window which opened upon a balcony was thrown up, — her friend gone!

"A very pretty cage, Margaret; but the bird is beyond your call."

Ralph's words in some degree aroused the failing senses of the stricken girl. Turning toward him, she said: —

"Ralph Bierce, tell me what you have done with Richard Whedden."

"I invaded the sanctity of your private apartment, Margaret, to find a woman; but, in her place, a sweetheart turns up."

"Ralph, answer me! you have a desperate woman to deal with; speak truly and quickly, or —"

"You will shoot me through the head. You have a fine weapon, a six-barrel revolver, by my life! Shoot away; a woman never hits!" *

"Does n't she?" A bat had flown in at the open window, and was wheeling in circles over their heads. As Maggie spoke, she raised her weapon; a sharp report followed, and the bat fell dead upon the newspaper, which Ralph held carelessly.

"By Jove! Margaret, practice will make you a killing shot."

The report brought Pomp into the room. He was a powerful negro, and powerfully armed, and no friend of Ralph's; that, the latter well knew. He glanced from the savage look of the athletic slave, to the mistress; her face, where beauty, purity, and dignity were so happily blended, was white as marble, and her eyes flashed intense indignation and stern resolve.

Ralph was unarmed; and, seeing that there was no way of escape, he said quietly, "Sit down, Margaret. I have to thank you for this timely discov-

---

* It may not be generally known that, at the commencement of this civil strife, the ladies of all ranks, and even children, practised, with pistols and revolvers, at marks, for the purpose, at first, of protection against their slaves, who became so saucy and impudent, it was hard to control them, — afterwards, it became a protection from insults from guerillas. — EDITOR.

ery, and will improve the present moment for doing so."

To her indignant response, he replied — " I found a man in yonder room; he said his name was Whedden, and I dropped him over the railing to my men below. If they have n't swung the scamp, he's —"

"Pomp, quick! follow these men, — there are but two, and you are a match for them. Save that man's life, and —" Maggie spoke in a sharp, quick voice, with her eye fixed on her cousin.

"Move one foot, nigger," burst in Ralph, but Maggie was too quick for him; she reached the door first. "Lock it!" she cried. The bolt slipped, and Pomp was safe without.

"Stand back!" Ralph shouted, but Maggie stood defiant and resolute. He looked at her, doubly armed, roused, as he afterward said, to perfect desperation; at the heavy door, securely bolted; at the open window, where he had so unceremoniously dropped a man crippled by a fearful wound; then, as no other alternative offered, he quietly walked back to his chair, and resumed his reading. An hour passed, and still another, and no sound broke the silence of the room, save the ticking of the clock on the mantel, and the monotonous turning of the leaves of the book, which Ralph held.

"Margaret," he said at length, "you have the spirit of a martyr," and, as he spoke, he turned and looked upon his captor. As no notice was taken of his remark, and he noted that her face had assumed a sternness, which showed that, in her nature, there was a strength of purpose not easily overcome, he spoke again; this time his voice was more gentle, almost persuasive.

"Yes, Ralph, you are in my power for this night, at least. By this time, Pomp has secured Mr. Whedden, and they have made good their escape, or he is in the hands of the military authorities. I will now release you on one condition."

"Name it."

"Swear, that you will not molest my servants further; that you will leave my house, and never set foot in it again."

"That, I cannot; for it is by order of the Vigilant Committee I am here."

"Then confine yourself to the lower rooms, until the order is revoked."

"I can promise that, my spirited cousin."

"And you will leave my servants unmolested?"

"Yes."

"Then go." Rising, she placed her revolver to the lock, and shattered it.

"For such clemency," Ralph said, as she flung wide the door, "I will tell you that, with you alone, rests the exposure of this most disgraceful affair. My men believe that this Whedden was found and brought here by myself. They will know nothing more, for I shall see to it that you are placed in the way of no further temptation. My word permits your having your servants; they will be under my surveillance, however. I would suggest rest," he added; "you look worn and pale; then, with a kindlier look than Maggie had ever seen on that stern face, he bowed, and left the room.

The following day, Maggie's servants were returned to her. Of them she learned that, the night of Mrs. Fay's flight, they had been called into Ralph's room; Ann first, when, finding she did not work rapidly enough, — a revolver was to be cleaned; he might want it, he said, — he called in Lizzie. The evident reluctance of both to work did not escape his observation; so, on leaving his room, he turned the key upon them. He was pacing the hall into which Maggie's door opened, doubtless to assure himself that, although the hour for the flight ripened, the night wanderer had not come forth, when the slipping of a bolt attracted his attention. Before the door was opened, he was before it, confronting his cousin, and heard her softly whispered caution, which so painfully precipitated unlooked-for events.

"All is plain now, Lizzie. I could not understand why Ralph should attempt violence, without some weapon about him. Had we followed you out, we should have escaped him, as you say you met him at the door of his room."

"But 'pears like, missis, gettin' out of de house was runnin' slam inter de vile critters on de outside. De Lord's ways is right; it am all his fixin' dat de woman should 'scape, 'case she hab chi'd'en; and de man taken, 'case he hab nobody ter fret for him."

"It may indeed be so, Lizzie; but my conscience tortures me with thoughts of what I might have done."

Hours lengthened into days, days into weeks, and Maggie watched in vain for Pomp's return. Had he been killed, or had he secured the prisoner and escaped were the questions which she asked herself many times during the day. Of Mrs. Fay she could get no clue; that she had reached Weltown safely, she was confident, as she saw the horse she drove, at the gate, the morning subsequent to her flight; but had she succeeded in eluding the wiles of the merciless foe which tracked her?

"Lizzie," said her mistress, during one of those long days of unrest, "I feel strangely nervous; sit by me, and sing one of those hymns which please me, 'I'm going home,' I like it, — sing that." Lizzie had a soft, pleasing voice, and always felt "proud like," when her mistress would be amused or comforted by her singing. Promptly she made the attempt to do Maggie's bidding, but "I'm going" was all that would come; she made a second effort, but with no better success. "O, pray, missis," she cried at length, "can't sing dat," and, tossing her apron over her head, in agony of grief she threw herself upon the floor at Maggie's feet.

Maggie was startled; her first thought was that some new calamity had come down upon her doomed house. Was Harry dead? it was but yesterday she had received word that he was alive. Was she to be arraigned before the Vigilant Committee as a Yankee sympathizer? the thought made her face white, but her spirit was bold.

Not long, and her gentle, persuasive words eased the throbbing aches of Lizzie's great, warm heart, and her sad tale of treachery and death was fully disclosed.

This is her story: Jake, her husband, whom Lizzie loved with her whole heart, whose freedom she had purchased with her mistress' money, and into whose ear she had poured all the troubles and trials of those dark days, was the *traitor!* He, it was, who had sought out Ralph Bierce, and told him what daily transpired beneath the mistress' roof, with the hope of ultimately obtaining the reward offered for the apprehension of the woman who had shot Bill White. She had told Jake that some one was under her mistress' protection; but, as she had promised, had never even whispered names, although Jake was always at her to do so. Pomp had never liked Jake, because he was a free nigger, and daily told him to go along back to the city, and not to be sneaking about there. He had been to Lizzie, and told her Jake was a no-account nigger, and he meant to tell his mistress, and was only deterred from doing so by her saying, if he made one complaint about Jake, she would burn his cabin down; but, after what Pomp had said, she kept her eye on Jake, and held her tongue, which so provoked him that he swore he would get another wife, and run off North. The night Pomp was to carry Mrs. Fay away, Jake dogged Lizzie's steps as she went to the stable to give Pomp orders, and he heard enough to convince himself that some work was to be done that night in the big house, and the exact hour. He tried to bribe Ann to tell him what it was; but she called him a fool, and told him to get out, — that he did n't know what he was talking about. Jake told Ralph what he had heard, and, as his assistants were out on a scout, he was sent to the city for aid. In attempting to overtake the cart which bore the man Ralph had dropped from a window to his men, Jake was overtaken by Pomp; he knew him, and swore he was at the bottom of the fuss, and should smart for it. Jake knew Pomp would keep his word, and therefore fired upon him. Pomp returned the fire, and Jake fell. At that moment some one sprung from the side of the road and called Pomp. The two talked a few moments, then struck off up the road together. Jake was picked up by Ralph's men the following morning, and, at his (Ralph's) orders, carried to Pomp's cabin. He knew he should not live long, and begged to see his wife; but that was refused him. One day Lizzie heard the guard say, "That's a mighty nice cabin where that nigger is, but he'll have no use for it many more days." She thought it must be Pomp who was dying, and set her heart on reaching him. She did so by treating the guard freely to whiskey, and found, not Pomp, but Jake, sick unto death. He told her what he had done, and wanted her to tell her mistress it was for money to get off North, which had made him so wicked. He wanted her to sing, "I'm going home to die no more." While she was singing, he fell asleep; and for fear of detection she returned to the house. The next day, when Ralph returned from the city, she heard the guard say to him, "The sick nigger is dead;" she saw him throw them money, and heard him say, "See to it he is decently buried!"

CHAPTER XXX.

UNEXPECTED FRIEND.

"I saw the Yankee prisoners," said Helen Bierce, while on a brief visit to her cousin Maggie, after a somewhat lengthy visit in Newbern.

"Those that were wrecked off Beaufort during the late gale, Nellie?"

"Yes; I saw them as they marched from the depot to the jail, and I must add, though a very mean-looking set of men, they walked manfully, yes, defiantly amid the crowd, which abused them roundly; afterward, through the kindness of Dr. Pill, I visited the jail, or rather, saw all I wished to of them from without the door."

"Dr. Pill?" said Maggie, with unaffected amaze; "How came he in Newbern?"

"That, I cannot tell you; I only know that he is there, and in attendance upon the prisoners, some of whom sustained fractures in buffeting the waves. He is a man every way worthy of such a trust, I should judge, from what I have heard Ralph say of him, and, where there are so many traitors, — we know our city is full of them, — too much precaution cannot be exercised in securing responsible persons for such positions. To think of our jail being broken open the day of the Butler panic, by some of these same shameless creatures, and Mr. Whedden, the arch-traitor liberated! I knew, Maggie, he was no common man; the few moments I saw him here convinced me of that. It is inexplicable how a person, endowed with the highest order of talent, can be so recklessly indifferent to the sacredness of truth, and be guilty of the most heinous of all sins, — that of counselling his fellow-men to the betrayal of their country!"

"Have your Newbern friends quite recovered from the Butler panic?" asked Maggie, wishing to avoid further conversation upon Mr. Whedden's escape.

"Yes, quite so, and, as you may well believe, are extremely sensitive upon that topic. What is intolerable to me is, that the men cast the odium which is heaped upon runaways upon woman's ever-convenient shoulders. Not one of them, but will tell you that their wives and little ones were their first care; and, safe abodes secured for them, with the first weapon at hand, they made all haste home to drive back the foe. But it is an incontestable fact that not a man was seen in citizen's dress in Newbern's streets, until square, street, and alley resounded with the martial tread of soldiers from Virginia."

"Missis is wanted," said Lizzie, approaching; "and the man says he has 'tickler business, and can't wait."

"Stay, dear Nell, till I return."

An hour later, and we will venture to look in upon the mistress of the house and the new comer, and we hear:—

"Are any of the prisoners very sick, Harry?"

"Dr. Pill, madam!" said the person addressed, with a frightful shake of the head.

"My third offense," laughed Maggie; "but I am so happy, so very happy, Dr. Pill, you must forget to scold. You can never deceive me again, never," she added emphatically; "if you make yourself ten times more hideous than you are now, and wear two wooden arms instead of one. And to think that it was through your agency that Ralph and his company were cut off from a retreat to the boats, and met the fate they deserved on the surrender of the forts. Dear, dear Harry! never did a heavier weight of trouble and dread fall from mortal shoulders, than from mine, when, on the list of Hatteras prisoners, I read Ralph's name. But tell now the particulars of your flight from the field, and your subsequent adventures."

"Not now, dearest, for my time is too limited for so long a tale;" then, glancing at his watch, "only a half-hour to the time for the evening train."

To Maggie's earnest entreaty, he resumed:—

"Let it suffice you, for the present, to know, that having heard through a brother-officer of the treatment you had been subjected to through Ralph's agency, I left my regiment at Manassas, and, having secured a complete disguise, returned here with the determination to dislodge the scoundrel. What my plans were to secure his person, and liberate Richard Whedden, I cannot now divulge; but the timely arrival of the Yankees upon our coast brought my project to an earlier culmination than my most sanguine hopes could have anticipated."

"Was it you, Harry, who hailed Pomp the night of Mr. Whedden's arrest?"

"Truly, it was none other, and it was my shot which sent that rascal, Jake, to his final account. Of Pomp, I learned of Mrs. Weasel's flight, and I despatched him to her assistance; and, as the long-looked-for time had not come, when I could safely, that is, consistently with all our interests, make myself known to you, I lent my entire energies to Mr. Whedden's demands. Through Dr. Hall's aid, who alone of my friends knew of my return, I had secured means for his escape from prison-walls, when that, to us, glorious Butler panic dispensed with further intrigue, and numbered Dr. Pill and friend among the ghostly throng which westward pressed."

"Well do I remember that memorable morning."

"And Miss Helen does, also, I reckon."

"Why, Helen? She, I was told, was the only lady in town that did not leave in the panic."

Then followed the particulars of the freak of his mule before her door, and his gaining the possession of his own horse, Nise, from her stable. Recovering her composure, which Harry's exploit had for a time completely overthrown, Maggie said:—

"Now tell me of your patients, the prisoners; are they very great sufferers?"

"Sufferers! Maggie, no. A more determined, unequivocal set of men cannot be found on God's footstool. Brandy and wholesome food are what they want to set them on their feet again. I am wrong, however, in saying they are all mending; there is one who is 'heavily under the weather.' He is a stranger to the others; they tell me, the first night of the blow an object was seen bearing down upon them, which proved to be a dismantled craft. No living thing was seen on her; and we think this man must be a survivor of the wreck, for he was picked up only a few hundred yards from the spot where the surf washed the others ashore. He has sustained some internal injury, I fear. Dr. Sharpy has my pass during my absence, and I depend upon his being able to help the poor fellow. Maggie," he added, feelingly, "I would not exchange the satisfaction of giving an encouraging word to these brave Yankees, for aught earth can offer; and, if I live, I will yet free every one of them, and you must aid me."

"I, Harry?"

"Yes. Newbern must be your home while it is mine; for I not only need your coolness and judgment to aid me in perfecting my plans, but I feel it is not safe for you to be longer here without a protector. The recent call for men for local defence assures me that not long, and our most sanguine hopes may be realized."

"You mean the advance of the Yankees into our State?"

"Yes; and God grant that the work they have to do here may be unflinchingly and thoroughly done! But what have you there, a letter?"

"Yes, from my dear young friend, Annie McGowan; it was handed to me as I passed through the hall."

"Read it aloud, Maggie. Her father is as true a Union man as we have in the State."

"You knew his son was in prison?"

"Yes, in Salisbury. I saw him there; he bears his captivity like a martyr."

"What talismanic charm opened those doors for you, Dr. Pill?"

"I got in, then got out again," said Harry, laughing at Maggie's evident astonishment at his ubiquity. "No more questions now, love, for I am anxious to hear the letter. I see in the papers, when the draft came off in Whiteville, there was considerable trouble; several arrests were made."

"When does the draft come off here?" asked Maggie, breaking the seal of her letter, and shaking the finely-written sheets into her lap.

"To-morrow."

"Will you escape the draft?"

"Of course, by being one of the medical board. Read now."

Maggie read : —

"My heart is almost broken. I shall feel better if I write, for, while I do so, I can hide my face from mamma. She is an angel, or she could not bear trouble such as ours, so heroically; while I — You shall hear what has befallen us; then you will pity, not blame.

"Poor, dear papa has been cruelly imprisoned; what will be done next? My heart shudders to think to what fearful extremities men like Calvin Hicks carry their malignity. I know I should die if I could not see papa. I go daily by the jail window; from behind those horrid bars, he looks out, and smiles so kindly, as if to say, — 'be patient, Annie.' I feel my heart has grown strangely cold and hard, and, only when I am practising with my pistol, Frank's last gift, do I lose the throbbing ache which sickens my soul. There is something in the smell of powder, in the sharp report, in the sight of the wood where I have buried my ball, which tells me, small girl that I am, I have power.

"Maggie, I have sent you my Diary for the past week; read it, dear friend, then come to comfort mamma.

"*Dec.* 1. Rode out with Mr. Wilson. We went to the camps; the entire town was there to see two Yankees, captured on the coast, then on their way to Salisbury. Secesh acted hatefully; but the Yankees appeared unconcerned, as if 'calculating' the chances of escape. Examined the Testament which saved the life of one of the prisoners; it was directly over his heart; the ball pierced the Book, but *glanced off* at the words, 'Who delivered us from so great a death, and doth deliver; in whom we trust that He will yet deliver us.' * The man escaped without a scratch.† Percy, after looking at the Book attentively, said: 'Miss Annie, God loves that Yankee, does n't he?'

"I caused one of the prisoners to look at me, by whipping my pony to a dance amid the crowd. He caught my whip, which I flung at him, and, when it was handed back to me, the paper I had wound around it was in the Yankee's hand. He read it; our eyes met, and we both smiled; he will know Frank now when they meet. On our ride home, we met fifty of our own soldiers marching to town, handcuffed. Oh, such a fearful sight! Fathers, brothers, sons, bareheaded, wan, and haggard, driven on in irons, to be shot, perhaps, or, what is less merciful, left to starve in prison. They were deserters,— nine months' men, who had served their time, and refused to re-enlist; and, to avoid being compelled to do so, run off.

"*Dec.* 2. Thirty of the prisoners, respectable men from our county, and many of whom papa knew,

---

* 2 Cor. i. 10.

† This fact was given the writer by the surgeon who examined the prisoner.

slept in our barn last night; sent to papa to feed, because a Union man. Sarah gave the guard whiskey, and, when they were completely stupefied, mamma and I went to the sufferers; we gave them brandy, and had their blistered feet washed. Mamma encouraged and prayed for them; I could only counsel them to take the arms I offered, and dispatch the guard. At sunrise, the men formed into line; 'March!' shouted the captain, and they passed from sight down the dusty road. I dare not write how I felt when I thought of the agonized hearts from which they had been torn by their savage keepers.

"*Dec.* 3. The day of the draft! Percy and I sat at the window to watch the people that thronged the streets. Blustering Secesh rides furiously up to the Court House; men, unconditional Unionists, walk erect and firm; 'If I am drafted, I won't go," can be plainly read on their faces. Scarey men, who want to save what they own, who are troubled to know which side is the strongest, which, in the long run, will hold out best, in great trepidation draw near to the boy with the box, who bawls out, 'Who's got to face the fire?'

"The crowd thickened, so did the dust; and Percy and I left our point of observation for the garden, to attend to the flowers and pets. A great noise came up from the Court House; we listened, it came again; it came so often, we at length forgot to notice it, — forgot everything but the vast improvements we were making in mamma's garden-beds. The sun set, then we watched for papa's steps; he said he should not dine with us, but early twilight would find him at home. Night came, and no papa;

supper was spread, but remained untasted. My heart whispered, 'patience! Calvin Hicks is away; no harm can come to papa.' Another hour passed, then a step was heard upon the walk. Mamma, Percy, and I were at the door; a negro was there. He handed mamma a note; she read it by the hall-light, then fell insensible. We restored consciousness; she bade me go to bed, and said in the morning I should know what troubled her. She looked so sad and sick, I could offer no remonstrance. After Percy fell asleep, I wrapt myself in a shawl, concealed my pistol in its folds, and stole noiselessly from the house to search for papa. I well knew where to turn my steps; for I read 'jail' in mamma's face. The jailer I knew to be a good man, and a Unionist. I reached his house; he received me kindly, but resisted all my entreaties to be admitted into our loved one's cell. With the promise that he would give him a note, that before many days I should go to him, I grew calm; but would not return home until I had heard what occasioned papa's arrest.

"'And it was Calvin Hicks that did it,' I cried.

"'Col. Hicks has no doubt helped this matter along, but, for many months, John McGowan's life and his friends' have been threatened. In such sorry times, you must be thankful nothing worse was done than shutting them up here, where, in my mind, they are safer than if in their own beds.'

"'They are irresponsible men, and may make it worse any time.'

"He made no reply, but I heard him mutter Calvin Hicks's name with an oath; he told me of the

19*

draft, — that those shouts which we heard were raised by Union men when Secesh were drawn.

"'The Lord's hand was in it, Miss Annie, for, of all the names drawn, Secesh outnumbered Union men, five to one. A row followed; the Unionists would have come off best, for the Rebs were just about 'done gone,' when Hicks and his squad rode up. He had a warrant to arrest John McGowan, Robert Wilson, Frank Graves, and some six others. This settled the fuss; the draft was declared unfair, and another is to come off next week.'

"I wrote my note, and left the house. I stood upon the door-step, and looked up to those gloomy walls, which shut from sight papa, and all those good men whose names the jailer had given me. Their wives and children must watch and wait; their hearts ache, as mamma's and mine, and must keep on aching until the Yankees come. Frank's words came to me: 'A woman armed is more formidable to meet than a man, when the sanctity of her home is invaded.' 'Frank is right,' I thought; 'women, nowadays, must study something beside patience; they must fight, and they can do it to save their loved ones from cruel deaths. Who,' I thought, 'had brought down upon us such misery? Who had sworn never to rest until Jane McGowan had drank to the dregs the bitter draught his malignity had concocted? You, Calvin Hicks!' I involuntarily shouted. I had gone to the gate; so shaken was I by the hateful thoughts, which tortured me, I had not noticed the approach of a horseman. At the sound of my voice, he drew rein, then walked his horse by the fence on which I leaned. The newly-risen moon shone fully on his face, so hideous, so sinister; my implacable enemy was approaching me! I did not feel in the least agitated; from the moment he told me of Frank's arrest, and I saw the triumph in his evil eyes, a violent wish seized me to avenge our wrongs. Now, when smarting from a blow heavier than the first, my merciless foe appeared before me. I knew I was in the shadow of the house; that, if seen, I could not be recognized; I felt those horrid eyes glare upon me, and I seemed to hear the glad chuckle hiss from his teeth, that another McGowan was in his grasp, and that victim my papa! The thought maddened me; I drew my pistol from the folds of my shawl, raised it, and took deliberate aim. As my finger pressed the trigger, he leaned towards me, and I heard, 'Is that you, Sal?' I heard no other sound; but I saw the tall man reel in his saddle, then strike the ground.

"I reached home. I spent the long night in the garden; I woke my pets, and fed them; I picked flowers for the vases, and, with my apron full, walked up and down the shadowy paths until morning broke; then I went to the house, to my own little room, and prepared for breakfast. As I write, I am calm. I shall meet mamma at the breakfast-table; will she remark my quietness, and read in my eyes what my hand has done?

"Night. The house is still; I can write now of this eventful day, then go to my watch. Mamma did not go down to breakfast; she was too ill. Sarah told me at the table that Col. Hicks had been shot dead by a negro, during the night. She said everybody in town was glad of it. I sent for John; he, too, said Col. Hicks had been shot. I asked him where? 'Near the jail,' he said; 'the guard heard the report of a pistol, and reached the spot where the Colonel lay, in time to see a negro running down the road. The man was not dead, but dying,' John said, and I dismissed him. Mamma called me to her room, and handed me the note which she had received the night before. I read it, but so calmly, she pressed me to her, saying: —

" 'My daughter does not distress me by her usual violent expressions; now read,' she added, ' this note, which has just been sent in.'

" I took the note; it was from the friend, who had sent news of papa's arrest. Therein I read of the mortal wound Calvin Hicks had received during the night, — supposed to have been inflicted by one of his negroes, who had once before attempted his master's life.'

" I could not speak; I bowed my face in my hands, and knelt down by mamma's bedside. ' Annie,' she said, ' while we may rejoice that God has removed from our path so violent an enemy, we must pray that he may be awakened to a sense of his own wickedness; that his last moments may be spent in making his peace with his Creator.' I made no reply, but kissed mamma, and left the room. I went to the jail; papa was at the window. He had read my note, — I saw it in his face. The jailer told me Col. Hicks had been shot down at his gate, not a half-hour after I left his house.

" ' Will he die? ' I asked.

" ' The chances are ten to one that he does; the wound has been probed, but, they tell me, the ball cannot be extracted. Ah! Miss Annie, you should hear how your papa and all the Union men rejoice that such a devil has been cleared from their path.

Mark my words; they will be free in less than ten days. 'Twas that man, Hicks, who kept the county in such a stir about them; and, I can tell you now, he swore he would have every one of them shot, or in Salisbury, before the week was out; and he would have made his threat good, if the Lord had n't put him out of the way.' To-morrow, he said, I should see papa; that, now Hicks was dispatched, there was not a man living he feared.

"The day has passed. As I kissed mamma 'good night,' I told her I was to watch with a sick person. She either did not hear, or was too engrossed with her own thoughts to heed my remark; for she smiled when I spoke, but did not question me. She is sleeping now; so is Percy, and I lay down my diary to go to duty as nurse.

"*Dec.* 5. Last night I watched with the sick man; no one comes to Calvin Hicks's couch, no one speaks of him but in terms of reproach; even the doctor looks in upon him as if he wished it might be his last call. What a dreadful misfortune to live, hated of all men! but what a terrible thing to die without raising one prayer for forgiveness! Throughout the night, I sat by his couch, and bathed his head, and cooled his swollen lips; while my ears were filled with the groans which his agony wrung from him. I knelt down at his side, and prayed that my sin might not be visited upon those I loved; that one short hour of consciousness might be allowed the sinking man for repentance. For myself I could not pray; I felt no contrition, no grief; I simply felt glad that Calvin Hicks, the guerilla chief, the wife-murderer, the fiendish captor of my father and brother, was powerless to commit further crimes, and, in his own body, suffering the torments he loved to inflict upon others. No suspicion of the deed would rest upon me, but I knew God's eye saw my heart, and from Him I felt my sentence must come. I left the house when day broke. I left him alone, for his servants, after robbing their master of everything valuable, had taken to the swamps; but, while he lives, mamma and I will see that he does not suffer for nursing.

"I go to the jail at ten o'clock. Oh! the joy, the delight, of being locked in papa's arms again! I shall tell him all."

Here the diary closed. Upon a slip of paper, inserted, was written : —

"The jail was empty! Papa gone, without one kiss, one embrace, one look! I can have no rest, no peace, until I track the murderers, and know — what would I know? — if papa is among the living. Maggie, I send you my diary by John; in mercy to poor mamma come back with him; she and Percy watch for you. I fold and send this with a kiss; before it reaches you I shall know somewhat of papa.
"ANNIE."

"DEAR MAGGIE : —

"Annie has left me with friends. She seeks news of her father. Return with my servant if you can; your sympathy may ease my heart, wrung with unutterable woe.
"JANE McGOWAN."

CHAPTER XXXI.

SCENES IN NEWBERN. — THE WINTER OF 1862.

THE season which followed the Hatteras alarm was the gayest ever recorded of the city of ———. Martial strains and martial sights filled the streets, and the lofty consciousness of "irresistible might," and duty unflinchingly met, the hearts which beat *en militaire*, and the more tender ones under calico and homespun. What though the blockade banished rich viands and Eastern luxuries? The guest was no less welcome at the hospitable board, and regaled with delicious decoctions of parched rye and sweet potato, which, sipped from china and silver, was pronounced more than a fair substitute for Java and Mocha. What though the salad was crude and unsavory, the light laugh and bewitching grace with which it was tendered, made the otherwise unpalatable bitter, sweetness. What though the hand which rested upon the gay cavalier was gloveless, how proudly it was pressed! Is it a marvel that the warm blush kindled, as upon the manly form at her side, the devoted maiden recognizes the suit which her own hand had woven, with its warp of gray cotton and woof of silk, — the very silk which once adorned that *petite* figure, cut, ravelled, carded, and woven by the hand which now, in happy confidence, is laid upon the arm, upraised in defence of Southern rights and Southern glory.*

At the height of the winter's festivities, a sound of warning came, which caused the revellers to lose the measure, the camp-weary to move as if there were fight and glory ahead, and the *triste* to look bold and defiant, — *all*, eager for the fray, if, to their shores, the prows of the "invincible armada," which had left Hampton Roads, should be turned.

"Formidable, invincible, indeed!" laughed the young Confederacy: "what had Southern braves to fear from a set of snivelling pettifoggers, pedlers, cobblers, and colliers, such as New England had turned out to equip Burnside's expedition, — the nine-days' wonder."

A hearty laugh is contagious; and the mere suggestion of this "far-famed expedition" called forth such commentaries upon New England Yankees, — which, in Secesh parlance, can be more becomingly imagined than repeated here, — that convulsive cachination was universal.

Poor, deluded chivalry! even while maniacly you hurl defiance at *Liberty's own*, their foot is on your shore. Back to your cotton-bags creep! Strip patch after patch, pile bale upon bale until their snowy crests pierce the clouds; cry aloud, Cotton is king! Cotton is mighty to save! — but hark! the upspringing breeze brings to your ears the thunder which heralds the *Conqueror come!*

Through the smoke of the black-mouthed cannon,

---

* A fact, that old black silk, cut in shreds, then carded, spun, and woven with cotton warp, will make a pepper and salt colored cloth, quite handsome. I have helped make this cloth, and know the suits have been worn. — AUTHOR.

faces, glowing with the indomitable confidence of power, look forth and shout; "Come with us! Come with us! Though your hands are defiled with blood, and your fingers with iniquity; your lips have spoken lies, and your tongue uttered treason; sheathe the sword! Take once more for your watchword, 'Liberty and Nationality;' then, "though your sins be as scarlet," they shall be forgiven you; "though they be red like crimson," they shall be washed white!

My people had eyes, but they would not see; they had ears, but they would not hear; but they *felt* the blows which struck Roanoke from their hands. Transfixed as with lances, they, gaping, stood, and beheld the "cobblers pegging," then broke, with the cry, "Abe's tigers are on us!"

Oh! the direful confusion, the unmitigated terror, the splenetic rage of the luckless ones who heard the wail:—

"The bars are down! The Yankees hold the State! Westward!"

And westward it was by night and day. Pack-mules, horses, ringed-boned, spavined, blind, and lame, with their living freight, filled the forests, and crowded the human stream which pressed on for middle Carolina. Mothers, with infants in their arms, plied the oar in leaky boats, under pelting rains, and suns which blistered little bare heads; for, in that terrible flight, hats and caps were forgotten.

The road by day, and the midnight escape, were alike illumined by the cotton conflagration; while the more vivid light of burning turpentine discovered *the thoughtful servant looking after massa's effects:*

"Run, missis, run! I'se lookin' arter things, and, quick as a wink, 'll catch up."

Mistresses ran; so did the Abigails, *but in opposite directions!* White hands, empty, — black and cunning ones, overflowing!

Newbern, intrenched behind her "impregnable forts," heard the rout, and paled, not with fear, but with anger, at the second laying-on of Yankee hands upon Carolina's soil. Among the fugitives which crowd the streets, we recognize many acquaintances from forsaken cities and towns on the coast. Not the least gay is Mr. Francis Bierce's household; not the least happy, Maggie Blout's temporary home, which is daily enlivened by Dr. Pill's jovial presence.

A bright March morning sees Francis Bierce pacing his office with agitated steps. His usual placidity of expression has vanished, and now heavy foreboding darkens his brow, and sets deep lines about his mouth. A friend breaks in upon his revery, exclaiming, "That was a capital speech of yours, Bierce, last night. Your patriotism will cost you something, sure."

"Not a cent," said the one addressed, drawing up his chair to his friend's side; "don't think I'm such an ass as to go down with this d—d Confederacy. I've secured a plank which will survive the wreck, and I reckon *you* are with me there, Dunn."

"Why, yes, my cotton I sold some weeks ago down in Georgia; but you told me, certainly not more than a week ago, you had some thousand bales on hand."

"Exactly! but I've sold it to a bale."

"And your turpentine?"

"Not a barrel of it in the State."

"That's neat for you; but, tell me, how did you bring about such sales?"

"I have friends in Congress, who do not mean to see themselves, or their supporters, brought quite to the wall; they initiate me into the ways and means of laying in for a wet day. This making a bonfire of property may be fun for Jeff's agents, but I'll be ———, they shan't set match to mine!"

"Things are looking bad for us, Bierce, mighty bad; it's hard telling what we are coming to."

"To my mind, Dunn, it is as plain as day that we are coming to h—l, every soul of us, through the perverseness and incompetency of that tyrant and fool, Jeff Davis. Why was our garrison crippled at Roanoke, just as the Yankees were on us? Why our own brave boys called out of the State, and South Carolina's sneaking d—ls sent here for our defence? What does Jeff care if our State is overrun with Northern Vandals, if he, and his army in Virginia, can fatten on our bacon, and fight from behind the ramparts which our boys' guns afford?"

"We are getting it! We are getting it! No doubt about that; and it comes of our letting the iron cool before we struck. Kentucky and Missouri brag 'their flags were flying, before the bunting of ours was woven. Jeff calls us a 'drag;' and, now that we have been twice whipped on our own soil, every State in the Confederacy cries, 'Cowards!'"

"Hang me! Dunn, if I would n't like to see Davis and his Confederacy sunk! Ah! how are you, Green? Glad to see you. Mr. Dunn, Judge Green. Any news for us to-day from your way?" asked Mr. Bierce, handing the new comer a chair.

"The 'Yanks' have fired our town.'

"That's bad, Green."

"I'll be blessed if I care a fig if they have razed it to the ground. *I've lost everything!*"

"Everything, Green? Not so."

"But it is so. Every nigger, every bale of cotton is gone! and, as for my wife and children, they might as well be in another planet for all I know of them;" and a heavy groan from the penniless, widowed boaster of the "Home," followed.

Again the door opened. "Bierce," said a bustling man entering, "couldn't leave the city without telling you what a heap of good your speech, last night, did me. I agree with you heartily, that a man is as much a traitor to his country, as a Yankee abolitionist, who refuses to put the brand to his cotton and turpentine. I'm off now to follow your example; if I have n't as many cotton bales by a hundred, I'm a little ahead of you in turpentine, I reckon. Our President, our cause, need just such men as you to keep us sharp to the mark. Publish your speech, Bierce; publish it in all the papers, and the Yanks may hunt the Confederacy through for a pound of cotton, or a gill of turpentine, to gloat over."

On the evening of the same day, Miss Helen Bierce's parlors were brilliantly lighted; for there, were assembled the grave, young and gay, who, with pleasing rivalry, vied with each other in the sprightly sally, and patriotic song, to drown the humiliating consciousness of the enormity of the disaster which had befallen their State. The presence of Gen. Runn and staff added much to the *eclat* of the occasion.

"General," said Helen, turning from the piano, where her brilliant execution of the "Manassas Rout," — the most popular piece of the day, — had elicited the warmest encomiums; "how many weeks have we to enjoy the undisturbed possession of this, our adopted city?"

"My dear young lady," was the reply; "you, like many others, and, I may add, the press universally, give the Yankees credit for a display of prowess they by no means deserve. Among the Yankee pioneers of the West, we may expect to find pluck and dogged obstinacy, naturally the result of the wild life they lead, which may give us some trouble to overcome; but Burnside's men are mostly New England Yankees, and, my word for it, not one in ten among them can handle a musket soldierly, if they can distinguish the breech from the muzzle."

"But you must allow, General," said Helen, "that they gained a decided advantage over us at Roanoke."

"Yes, some little advantage; all owing to their great superiority in numbers, however. Let them follow the '*ignis fatuus*' which has led them on thus far, and they will find Newbern a bog from which there is no escape."

Respect, paid to the opinion of superior officers, silenced further remark upon the subject of Yankee capacity. Glances, however, were exchanged amid the crowd of eager listeners, and more than one eye flashed saucily, as if something might be said to the contrary, if to disagree with so wise a General was not unpardonably discourteous.

"Then we are free from all alarm here," Helen said, glancing mischievously upon the group around; "this leaving home in a panic is distressingly unsightly, to say the least."

"Laugh at us, Helen, if it so please you; we all know your courage, and the fact, also, that it was only at the command of your father, you left. As for myself, I am not ashamed to own I was among the foremost to run from home at the Butler scare, nor to avow that, at the present time, I feel quite in the mood for ruralizing, although the season for the country has not begun."

To a remark of one of his staff, Gen. Runn replied: —

"Certainly, certainly, the possession of our inland seas is of some advantage to our enemies, but not, as many think, an irreparable loss to ourselves. With the force assigned me, I feel confident we shall sustain no further loss, and shall ultimately drive the invaders from the State."

"I have never seen a Yankee, and hope I never may, was whispered, as the General, bowing, moved away; "but I must believe them brave, for our soldiers, those that escaped from Roanoke Island, say that of them."

"Who have you seen from there, Miss Jennil?" clamored a dozen voices.

"Richard Smith, one of Gen. Winder's staff; and you may believe it or not, but he says the Yankees marched up to our batteries, as if *rations*, not grape and canister, awaited them. To use his own words, 'Burnside's boys are no cowards; the very music they step out is, "Clear out: those guns are ours."'"

"What you repeat may be substantially true; coming from such a reliable source, we must give some credence to it; but, when opposing forces were so fearfully disproportionate, we must not mistake strength for valor."

Said another of the group, "The Yankees have

not shown themselves the proletarians we thought them. Here comes the Captain Selden; he is honest and outspoken; we will hear his opinion of the invaders."

"What is it," asked that officer, drawing to the side of the young lady who beckoned his approach; and, to her question, replied: —

"Donelson and Roanoke afford fair proof of some ability, surely."

"But that does not satisfy us, Captain. We wish to know, if man to man the North and South should meet, which do *you* think would come off victorious?"

"Miss Jennil, I have never met our enemy in the field; until I have, I cannot give you a fair opinion."

"Nor never will, so long as your company is stationed here."

"It is by no means unlikely that your city will be attacked."

"Burnside is too prudent a general to lead his men upon such fortifications."

"It may prove so; but say, ladies, to look the matter full in the face, are you prepared for any emergency which may arise in case Newbern is attacked!"

"You surely do not mean to insinuate there is further flight for us, Captain?" said the startled Jennil.

All present, in fact, the entire State, knew that, from the first incursions of the Yankees under Butler, by unremitting toil and at enormous expense, Newbern had been rendered, to use the popular word, "impregnable."

"For," said the press, "if the fall of Hatteras, and, more recently, the surrender of Roanoke Island, should be followed by the loss of Newbern, a great portion of the State, embracing the most valuable lands, wealth, and, at least, one third of the slave population, would then be in possession of the enemy."

So, by every scheme which human ingenuity could devise, the channel of the Neuse was blocked, that the approach to the city might not be made by gunboats; and water batteries and field fortifications reared a threatening front for miles around. The idea, therefore, of Newbern's falling into the hands of the foe, was simply absurd; and the Captain's suggestion of a thing so improbable elicited general and hearty laughter. The quick eye of Miss Jennil, however, caught the slightly significant smile which the Captain cast upon the ladies, ere he turned away. It was too transient to admit of comment; but how forcibly it came back, when that ride of forty miles to Kinston found her fleeing from shot and shell, — the ravishing flames of her own home lighting her flight! But this is anticipating.

A glad cry drew the attention of the thronged parlors to the hall. Through the open door their radiantly beautiful hostess appeared, leaning on the arm of a tall, dark stranger. A second glance assures us we are right, and, with the crowd, we exclaim, "Ralph Bierce!" The exchanged Hatteras prisoner was returned.

RAILROAD BRIDGE ON FIRE.

CHAPTER XXXII.

THE RAILROAD BRIDGE SET ON FIRE.

Newbern is situated at the confluence of the Neuse and Trent rivers. The latter is spanned by a railroad bridge, the most extensive and, by far, the most costly structure of the kind in the State. It was the prevailing opinion that Beaufort, a pleasant seaport town, not many miles from Newbern, would be the next place attacked by the invaders; and, as this bridge afforded transit for troops and army supplies for that town, as well as the chain of forts above and below, it was necessary that great caution should be exercised to preserve it intact. It follows, therefore, that a strong guard and heavy ordnance defended its several approaches.

We have left the brilliant *coterie* at Mr. Bierce's dwelling; and, as the midnight bell is arousing distant echoes, we stand upon the shore of the dark Trent, watching a skiff which, with muffled oars, drops silently down its unruffled waters. The small boat hugs the east shore, and, in the friendly shadow of the overhanging trees, escapes the tell-tale beams of the moon, which, now in her first quarter, hangs low in the west.

The boat nears the bridge, and, for a moment, the oarsman lifts his paddle: but no sound save, "Who cooks, who cooks," from an owl on the woody shore, breaks the night's stillness.

The watch sleep on their post!

The wary adventurer strikes the water once, twice, thrice; still, no sound comes from the sound sleepers, which the slanting moonbeams display stretched upon the earth, or, with heavy heads hung low, studying repose with arms locked about muskets, as if danger threatened *them*, not the proud superstructure which bridged those placid waters. The boat now glides boldly out; but is soon lost to sight in the shadow of the middle pier.

A half-hour passed, and the sentinel upon the city shore stops his measured tread to gaze upon his comrade. Over his face, which his hand supports, (for the soldier had thrown himself upon a pile of timber near,) a bluish light plays. It lights up the grass, trees, and, even now, is reflected from the tall spires and windows of the city.

The guard leap to their feet, and, upon the night air, rings out sharp and shrill, "Fire! fire! The bridge! the bridge!" Wildly ring the bells; firemen spring to their engines, to find the hose punctured and wholly useless! and the wind is rising! By the flames, which spread slowly, a surging mass of beings, appalled by the overwhelming ruin which the destruction of the bridge threatens, is seen nearing the shore. And now, above the clamor of the crowd, the crackling flames, and rushing wind, rises the startled cry, "The Yankees are on us."

Eyes, distended with fear, see Yankee gunboats adown the river, and ears are horrified by screeching shell from out the iron monsters. Mute, terror-smitten, the tide of human life sways back to the city. Horsemen with fixed bayonets dispute the way. "To the bridge, fools! Cut down the cowards!" cries a bold man, charging his horse upon the foremost of the struggling mass; "to the bridge, or we are lost! Not a d—d Yankee in sight!"

The crowd part before the intrepid dragoon; his fiery words, his mad gallop to the scene of action, staggers them; they waver, they turn, and now, at double quick, rush to the shore.

One glance is flashed down the Trent; glowing in the rioting flames of the burning bridge; *grim phantoms* have *vanished!*

Daybreak sees the flames mastered; and men, faint, scorched, smoked beyond recognition, but exultant, that their efforts have saved the bridge, move down the city's streets, homeward. Maggie Blout had passed a sleepless night. From her window, she had been a calm observer of the burning bridge; as the last flame died out, she hid her face in her hands, exclaiming, " All is lost!" and the low droop of her head spoke of great despondency, almost utter despair. In the morning paper she read of the unparalleled audacity of the midnight incendiary; that, had he accomplished his fiendish deed, the forts below and their garrisons would have fallen, without a struggle, into the power of a merciless foe; that it was Yankee sympathizers, and the city swarmed with them, who had disabled the engines, raised the cry of " Yankees," and freed the teeming prison.

Farther down, her eye caught a name which caused her breath to come quick and short; and a whiteness overspread her face as she read: " To the self-possession and keen sagacity of Ralph Bierce, one of the returned Hatteras prisoners, who came in the evening train, is our city indebted for its rescue from the overwhelming ruin which threatened it in the loss of the railroad bridge. Well-mounted, he dashed his horse from the shore, when the cry of "Yankees" paralyzed the crowd, and, with the prison guard, that had secured horses from a stable near, met our frightened citizens, and, by his effective threats and noble example, calmed their frenzy, and turned them back to their duty."

That day, and for a week, a vigorous search was instituted for the perpetrator of the diabolical act of firing the bridge. The result of the search was a boat, picked up a mile down the river; but the combustible fluids, the tarred rope, and a well-worn straw hat, found therein, told no tales.

CHAPTER XXXIII.

MAGGIE IN PRISON; FINDS A SICK SOLDIER.

In a low, comfortless room, where, through chinks in the ill-matched boards which barred the window, dusty sunbeams wandered, we next meet Maggie Blout. She, too, was a victim of the relentless persecution which inaugurated Ralph Bierce's reign as Provost Marshal.

Men of law, letters, and religion, had been rudely seized, and, without the slightest investigation of the charges brought against them, cast into prison; it was enough that suspicion marked them as Yankee sympathizers. In the loathsome cell, on the straw pallet, dividing the coarse food, which was thrown at them as if they were indeed kennelled dogs; bearing all things, hoping all things, these brave souls, with unflinching spirit, sustained the torments of the day; for the light, which led on *advancing columns*, pierced prison gloom, and awoke in them that heroic endurance which bears witness of the "Godlike that is in man."

Maggie had heard of her many friends who had been forced to exchange the felicitous delights of the home circle, for the suspense and incurable aches of prison-life; and, when her summons came, she was ready.

Throughout her interview with Ralph, she sustained her usual quiet and becoming dignity, coolly parrying his questions where she, herself, was concerned, and resolutely refusing to utter one word, when commanded to disclose what she knew of the " spy," Dr. Pill.

" Yes, Margaret," he said, that Dr. Pill was a Yankee spy, and the villain, or one of his accomplices, who cut adrift the boat in which we were to make good our retreat, in case Fort Hatteras surrendered. A man, answering to his appearance, was seen by Helen on the day of the panic, making good his escape after robbing our stable of Harry Blout's mare; he afterward came to this city, and, by the most adroit duplicity, palmed himself off upon the Vigilance Committee, as a surgeon disabled in the Bull Run affair, and secured a pass to the Yankee prisoners, as medical attendant. *With them*, he has disappeared; and there is no longer any reason to doubt he has accomplices in our midst, who drugged the men detailed for sentinel duty the night of the fire, and then cleared the way for his own and prison-friends' escape. His coat and boots, which none other but a Yankee clodhopper could wear, have been found on your premises."

"The Yankees are reckoned a 'particular cute nation,'" was Maggie's reply, in no way disconcerted by the searching look which Ralph fixed upon her.

" Speak, Margaret, and tell me what you know of this Yankee spy, or your traitorous deeds shall cost you your liberty, — your —" he stopped.

" Go on, Ralph," was the calm rejoinder; " you would not hesitate to hang any of the men you have arrested on suspicion of loyalty to the Federal Government; and can I, whom you *know* to be unconditionally loyal, expect clemency of you, who sunk to the lowest depths of infamy when you swore fealty to treason's instigators."

"The undisturbed seclusion of the apartments which I have assigned you, and simple diet, may, possibly, temper your bold speech, Margaret; I will see you again to-morrow."

He tapped for a subordinate, and that official followed Maggie to the carriage in waiting. "The Whitney House, Elm St.," he shouted to the driver, and the carriage rolled away.

The third day of her imprisonment, which, Ralph said on his last visit, promised to be a long one, Maggie detained the negro keeper, and obtained the following information: —

"After a week's labor, the bridge would be passable; that everybody seemed to be in a mighty hurry, as if something was going to happen; that men on the street said, 'A week more, and, if attacked, we shall be able to give the Yankees particular fits;' that several arrests had been made the past two days, and sent off Kinston way; and that the man who groaned so in the next room was a sick soldier from Beaufort, who had been dying a long time, and, as the money was all gone, he would be nursed no longer."

Maggie watched that night with the sick man; and, as, by the dim light of a wretched "tallow dip," she gazed pitifully down upon the ghastly face of the sufferer, it seemed to her that every breath he drew served to hasten dissolution.

"Poor man!" she exclaimed, as she moistened his parched and shrunken lips; "such suffering as yours must atone for the sin of treason." The first hours of the night, the soldier moaned and tossed, as if in great pain: and, as Maggie had done all her limited resources allowed for his relief, she sat down upon the hard floor beside the pallet, and, to sustain her own fainting heart, sang a low chant.

The paroxysms of pain grew less violent, and, before the strain was finished, the soldier lay motionless. At first, Maggie could not realize the magical effect of her chant; then it occurred to her that she had read instances where music had been resorted to to soothe the last agonies of the dying. On the burden of her melody had that poor soul winged its flight? She hoped so; but no, there was a feeble pulse, and the chest moved lightly as in natural sleep. "So sweet a sleep will prove a salutary remedy; the sick man may yet live to make glad some watching, aching heart," she thought, and turned away.

Upon the roof the rain fell in torrents, and patter, patter, came the drops upon the wretched floor. As Maggie placed the saucer which held the "feeble dip," beyond the flow of the rivulets streaming from the broken ceiling, the sick man moved, and, as his nurse bent over his pallet, "Sing," came faintly. She sang some plaintive melodies, sweet and low, so low at last, it was as if an angel whispered. Maggie slept.

"Margaret!"

The watcher's sleep was broken; she sprung to her feet, exclaiming, "Here;" but, for the sweeping gusts without, she could scarce hear her own voice. "Some one spoke my name," she thought; "Harry is near!"

The window, if she could have found it in the dark, (for the sickly dip had succumbed to the rain-drops,) was too high for her to reach; that had not escaped her quick glance, on entering the room; and, as there was no other way of communicating with persons without, she contented herself with listening, oh, so wistfully! that the voice might sound again. But it came no more.

The dreary silence, which dragged the hours of the following morning, was broken by the thunder of artillery.

"They are but trying their guns at the forts," the watcher in the Whitney House sighed; and her hands, which she had clasped in an ecstasy of delight, as the report, so loud, so near, brought her to her feet, with the shout, "They have come at last!" dropped to her side, and again she sank upon the floor.

"Who have come, the Yankees?"

As Maggie turned to reply, she met the wild stare of the soldier, who had been roused by the guns, and was now supporting himself upon his elbow. The light from the window fell full upon both faces; their eyes met. The sick man's, then unnaturally brilliant, suddenly dilated with irrepressible joy; a convulsive twitching of the lips followed; then his outstretched, trembling arms sank down, his eyes closed, and he fell back upon his pallet.

"Poor creature!" sighed Maggie, as she sprung to his side, and looked down upon his face, stamped with the rigidity of death; "can it be there is life and hope for you, in the coming of the Yankees?" As she spoke, some sudden thought made her scan closely the white, gaunt face before her.

"It is the Yankee soldier," she cried; the one

Harry said must die; but how could so benevolent a heart permit this poor soul to be so neglected?"

The door of the room was, at this moment, swung open violently. "Quick, missis, quick!" her keeper shouted; "them's Yankee guns. Hear 'em bust! Gol-ee, what a big one!"

Before Maggie could offer any remonstrance to the movement, she was thrust into the apartment assigned her; she saw that her daily food was spread, and she knew that the closing door must debar her, for another long day, from intercourse from without. Quickly she drew, from the folds of her dress, her watch, and shook it before her excited keeper. As if struck with a magician's wand, the door stood wide open.

"Dat ar is a real beauty, sure. What does missis want for dat?"

"A doctor, medicines, and some clothes, for the sick soldier, Dinah, and it is yours. See, these are diamonds; some one will buy the watch of you, and give you a handsome sum for it."

Dinah held out her black, bony hand; while her hideously ugly face glowed with the exultant joy which the possession of such a trinket could alone excite.

"The doctor and medicines, first, Dinah."

The eager hands fell, and a scowl heightened the habitual repulsiveness of that brutal face; while, in the deep gutturals of her race, she muttered: "Now, dis minit! White folks tink niggers cheat."

"You, Dinah, do as I bid you."

The tone and the resolute eye, which denoted the custom to command, had the desired effect.

"Yees, missis, Ise off;" and the heavy door banged to behind her.

CHAPTER XXXIV.

13TH MARCH, STORMING THE FORTS. — 14TH, FALL OF NEWBERN.

ALL through the day, to the music of shrieking shells, men formed, and ready stood for the conflict. Night came, and there was no attack. Couriers from the forts brought to the city, deserted by all but women and children, the news that the foe were drawing back, staggered by the formidable barriers which disputed their approach; and a general feeling of disappointment prevailed.

Hatteras Inlet and Roanoke Island had fallen into Yankee hands, because of criminal delay on the part of *somebody*, — that universal author of all mischief. But now, when all things were ready, " with their backs to Dixie, the foe fled."

It was a bloodless victory; the proud city stood unscathed by shot or shell! " No prisoners, no trophies," and the crowd, which had thronged from town and country to see the fight, sighed heavily.

Our attention is particularly attracted to an old man, who had seated himself upon a fallen door-step. Two hundred miles from home he had wandered, to see the Yankees, and their " terrorscopic (telescopic) guns, which brought Dixie boys slam up to the muzzle, and dropped 'em dead without makin' a noise." And as, with sunset, the firing ceased, the last hope died out; and a tear dropped down the pilgrim's cheek, for the thought, that the tale to be told the loved mate, watching afar, of "Yankees caught, and the particular new gun," was as dry as the hoecake in the bucket by his side.

With the rising sun came the din of battle, loud, fierce, and terrific. High noon saw Newbern a city of prodigious confusion, and of wild turmoil; in broken ranks, and bleeding columns, her men line the shore, crowd the bridge, and flee the city's streets, in that unparalleled flight to Kinston.

From the stifling smoke of a burning house, Lizzie has drawn her mistress. Partially revived, she lays in her servant's arms, but wholly bewildered by the strange sounds, and burning sights, around.

Lizzie points to the house from which they had just made their escape, exclaiming: "See, missis, it's all fiery; it's goin'. Tank de Lord you ain't thar, nor nobody." With a look at the burning house, full consciousness returned, and Maggie sprung to her feet.

"There's a soldier there! He must not die; follow me!"

"Hain't nobody thar," and Maggie was held back by strong arms.

With a violent effort, the frantic girl tore herself from her servant's grasp, and turned towards the Whitney House, but her flight was impeded by the soldier's cot, which lay directly in her path.

"Me left nobody in dat ar house, to be burnt up, missis."

"Thank God, Lizzie; but is he dead?" and she bent down to the pallet.

"Only stuffed wid smoke, missis.

"Take him home, Lizzie; for the city will soon be completely consumed. Go quickly, and you will reach the shore road before the Yankees come up. See! the bridge is already in a light blaze; fortunately the wind blows from the house."

"Missis ain't got no home; 'tis burnt!" and tears washed the dusky face, which, with her concluding words, she hid in the soldier's blanket.

"Burnt!" was the startled reply; but, even as Maggie spake, the color came back to her cheek, and a triumphant smile lighted her face, as, pointing to the square, where the "stars and stripes" had just been flung to the breeze, she cried: —

"That sight is more than the wealth of the whole world to me!"

"All's gone, missis, but de kitchen," Lizzie said, raising her head, and gazing wonderingly at the new flag, — the flag which made her mistress smile, when she had not where to lay her head.

"Take him there, then; I will follow directly."

The sight of the black heavens, and the sweeping flames, bursting from every quarter of the fired city; the flight of a tyrannic host, commingling with the thundering shouts of victorious bands, which swept up the Trent's shores, was, to the lone watcher on the church's steps, supremely, awfully grand. Awe, adoration, and intense joy filled her soul; while ecstatic rapture burst from her lips, as, amid the smoke and battling flames, her eye again caught sight of the nation's ensign tossing high its broad folds, where, an hour before, treason's flag flaunted defiantly.

Imminent danger from cinders and falling rafters warned Maggie that she must not longer tarry. With a celerity of which she was herself unconscious, she sped down the river road, hoping to gain a woody bank ere hemmed in by Yankee soldiers, to whom the burning bridge was no barrier; for they were fast putting off in boats from the opposite shore. The bank is near; Maggie has reached it, and so has another, — a bleeding soldier, struggling with death.

Her woman's nature is at once aroused; and, forgetting all personal danger and discomfort, from blazing bridge-beams falling near, she stays her speed, and bends down pityingly over the sufferer.

With a start of surprise, she raised his wounded head, and tenderly wiped the blood from his pain-distorted features, but no other emotion escaped her, as, plainly, she recognized the familiar lineaments of her bitterest enemy, — Ralph Bierce. One glance assured her that his life was fast ebbing from a gun-shot wound in the neck; one arm was gone, and his clothes, torn and shotted, were stern reminders of the invincible spirit, which still wrestled in the flesh.

Knowing that her strength was not sufficient to secure for her charge, who, though fully conscious, was unable to aid himself, the protection of a tottering shed which was near, she concealed him behind a clump of cedars of low growth, and knelt down by his side to watch the triumphant approach of the battle-worn, blue-coated victors, as on, and on they came, making the welkin ring with pæans of victory. A groan, which the tortured man could not wholly suppress, met Maggie's ear; and her heart, whose wild pulse-beats were clapping a voiceless welcome to her country's defenders, melted at once to pity.

Her resolution was taken. A soldier had left the press, and, slackening his speed, was walking within a few yards of the secreted ones. "Ralph, if your enemy is as humane as brave, he will not refuse you aid; for myself, I have no fear; a valiant soul cannot be without honor." As she spoke, she stepped within sight, and motioned the straggler to approach. He sprang to her side.

"Soldier, —" she stopped abruptly; then grasped rapturously the extended hand; for, reader, this soldier, so buoyantly happy with the day's victory, was none other than Charles Coxe.

To Maggie's earnest inquiries concerning the friends who had escaped with him, she learned of their safety among unionists under Federal protection.

"Harry Blout, what of him?" she eagerly asked.

"He is here to answer for himself," shouted a voice from behind.

Maggie's start of delight, when turning she recognized Harry, and the warmth of their greeting showed how strong was their mutual affection.

CHAPTER XXXV.

THE FLIGHT FROM NEWBERN TO KINSTON.

" By my life, sir, those are particular loud guns," and so all the crowd thought, which thronged Kinston depot the morning of the 14th of March.

" A mistake, certainly, to think the Yankees could be frightened away by sight of our forts; they are trying them, it seems."

" Have you any boys in the fight?" asked a gentleman approaching the speaker.

" I hope so."

" How many?" cried out a watcher down the road.

" Four, as particular brave boys as you can find the Confederacy through."

" In what forts?"

" Two in Dixie, and two in Lane; they 're having some sport this morning, I reckon; its what they have been mad after, and now I hope they 'll fix the things up *handsomely*. " Have you seen our forts below?" questioned the proud father, complacently rubbing his bearded chin.

" I am a stranger in these parts."

" Going down with us, next train, to see the dogs kennelled, eh?"

" It is my purpose to go to Newbern. What hour does the train leave?"

" Four o'clock. She 's due here now in ten minutes. Shall have glorious news by her!—glorious!"

"What force is Burnside supposed to have below?"

"Forty-thousand, not a man less."

"And we?"

"Why our forts are worth to us double that number of men; and, sir, if the Yankees have been foolhardy enough to attack them, overwhelming defeat will be the result."

"To judge by sound alone the Yankees have made something of a stand."

"Shelling the woods, shelling the woods to cover their retreat. It takes a mighty sight of such music to set them up for a fight, and a heap more to call them back to the black devils."

"Then yesterday's cannonading was shelling to protect the landing of the troops?"

"Exactly; we about here thought the attack had been made and given up; it was a mistake, however."

"Burnside seems to be a cautious general; he moves slowly enough, certainly."

"There's not much fight in the man anyhow; he's got a fair office and fair pay, and he can't very well help fighting 'so, so,' when we give him so good a chance as we did, at Roanoke. You've heard what the boys say of him?"

"I see by the State papers he treats his prisoners handsomely, and in one of them, I think, I saw stated that he gave a dinner party, where our boys and the Yankees mingled promiscuously; and that, to some of our officers he remarked, 'he had no heart for such an unchristian war; that Massachusetts and South Carolina had kicked up the row and should fight it out among themselves.' That, however, is newspaper trash; I dont believe a word of it."

"Don't believe it? sir,—I've seen the man, who heard him say it."

"Just so. I, also, have seen several who indulge in very extravagant talk; the taller the story, the bigger the hero, usually. I would like to know if Burnside was graduated at West Point or no?"

"A West Point graduate!—no. Like 'Brute Butler' he was a down-east lawyer, second-rate at that.'"

"But we must acknowledge, as General commanding, his first strike was n't a bad one for him."

"Circumstances were not in our favor at Roanoke, certainly, but let me tell you, Newbern is a shoal for Burnside and his men, which wrecks the whole of them!"

"I see we differ essentially in our estimate of Burnside's ability. I will acknowledge, that his success at Roanoke led me to infer Newbern might succumb to his creditable skill and energy; and at the risk of being taken."

"What, sir, what! Newbern taken! Newbern, the Gibraltar of the Atlantic coast, captured by these Yankee marauders! By my life, sir, the idea is —" The speaker checked himself, and, drawing up to the stranger, took him by the buttonhole, saying, "You told me you were unacquainted in these parts. I believe it, sir; I believe it. We go down together in the evening train, and it will give me infinite satisfaction to show you some of our works below, built without regard to expense or labor; then, sir, you will acknowledge that they are impregnable!" Raising his head, and drawing himself up to his full height, he added: "Show me the general, show me the men, who can raze one stone of that city yonder, (pointing in the direction of Newbern,) and I will prove —"

The sentence was unfortunately lost, and the whistle of the approaching train effectually silenced further conversation.

The train swept up, — and on! at a rate of speed quite as unprecedented, on that road, as the event of Kinston being overlooked as a way-station. Cries that the engineer was mad, or drunk, burst from the now terribly earnest throng, and a general rush was made to the telegraphic office, to notify the stations ahead, of the coming train. After an hour of fearful suspense, a second train appeared. The shrieks of women, the groans of wounded soldiers, and the bitter, bitter lamentations of panic-stricken fugitives, heralded the *fall* of *Newbern!*

Had the heavens been rent in twain, had the seventh trumpet sounded the end of all things earthly, more appalling consternation could not have congealed the blood, and set the features of the lookers-on rigid as death, than did the cry, "The Yankees are in Newbern!"

A young soldier, lively and pert, sprung from the cars, shouting —

"Newbern's done, gone! Yanks hold Newbern! No need of a scare, women and children; it's an hour yet 'fore they'll be here!" then, clapping his hands into his pockets, he struck for town, whistling "Dixie," vehemently.

"My son!"

"How d'y, old man?" and the happy father of the morning pressed to his heart *one* of his "four brave boys."

"Newbern's done, old man."

"God's wrath is on us," groaned the trembling parent, supporting himself by placing both hands upon the boy's shoulders; "but where's Hal, Dick, and Johnny?"

"You see there was a mighty long run 'fore us, and, as I'm reckoned a fast one in the chase, I outstripped our brigade to a man, and got to the cars in the nick of time."

"The Yankees are pushing on this way?" was the trembling query.

"I reckon they are that; but don't be so scary; you are as shaky as them women yonder. There's no way of escape now but to take the next train for — for — I'm beat to know where a fellow can crawl, where 'Yanks' can't worry him! It's prodigious fits they've givin' us to-day; that's so."

"Where's your gun, boots, cap, boy?" asked the father of the panting heart, who, rejoicing in pants and shirt, thought a whole skin, a fair exchange for supernumeraries left on the wind.

"It's particular little use such traps are, to a fellow who looks to his legs for his life. I tell you what, there's mighty spoil for the ' Yanks,' on the road between here and the forts!"

A prolonged shout down the road was at this moment heard, which caused the pulse of Kinston to stand still; while eyes, distended with horror, vainly strove to pierce the heavy dust-cloud which marked the approach of coming horsemen. It lifts at length, and, *not Burnside* and his *unconquerable legions* appear, but *Gen. Runn*, his staff, and a goodly number of men, on bleeding, foam-flecked horses, in the mad gallop for life!

CHAPTER XXXVI.

ANNIE M'GOWAN'S LETTER. — A FRIEND IS FOUND.

Annie McGowan's letter to her mother at Salisbury: —

"Newbern, May 1.

"Cousin Harry — he insists upon my claiming that relationship — leaves here with a flag of truce, to-morrow, for Secessia. He goes to seek a dear friend, a Mr. Whedden, whom he concealed, somewhere in the western part of the State, from the rage of the Rebels. He says, 'write what you please, and as much,' that no eye but your own shall see it, mamma, for he gives it into your own hand.

"Dear, dear mamma, not an hour in the day but your image fills my heart, and I dream of you nightly, ever watching for one glimpse of papa and Frank from behind prison doors. But, mamma, our people will soon look up, and be free! for *Burnside is coming!* he is! he is! You, and Percy's mamma, must whisper the glorious news to loved, imprisoned ones, and to all hearts faint with watching and waiting for him.

"They tell me I am too sanguine; that it will take time, and a greater army than Burnside has here, to reach Salisbury. I cannot I will not believe it, for did not the General say to-day, — when some

Newbern ladies sought permission of him to accompany the flag, which goes to Kinston to-morrow, — 'Patience, ladies. I can promise you the escort of my army as far as Raleigh, in a few days.'

"One of the party said she made answer: 'If we wait for you and your army to escort us to our kin-people, we shall be palsied with age, and leprous from contact with creatures purgatory would refuse to hold.' Harry tells me no such reply was made; that one lady with a saucy toss of her head, said —

"'What right, Gen. Burnside, have you and your army here? debarring us —'

"'The right of conquest, madam,' said the General, interrupting; and, with a motion of his hand, he intimated that the interview was over.

"Harry declares he shall go on with Burnside and his army; and that no hand but his own shall knock the bolts from the Bastile at Salisbury, and bid loyal souls come forth to welcome the old flag and its plucky defenders. He is to plant the flag which I have made upon the smoking stones of the prison; for it is to be burnt to the ground, and not one stone is to be left upon another, to prate of the suffering braves once shut out from the living world by so fiendish a clique of Guy Fawkeses as are now struggling for unlimited power.

"And now you shall hear Maggie's secret, — 'that one thing secured, which makes her happiness complete.' This it is; Captain Carver, whose acquaintance Frank and I made while North, is here! and owes his life, he says, to Maggie, to whom he was betrothed some years ago!

"Thus the conjectures of the world, that the devotion of the cousins would result in ultimate union, are dissipated by the reappearance of the one long mourned as dead. And, if the astounding discovery, that the Yankee prisoner was none other than Captain Carver, Maggie's *fiancé*, whom, report said had paid the terrible debt to fate, while cruising on the African shore, has robbed Harry's heart of a dearly cherished hope, no act, no word of his will publish it, further than what he said to me, when speaking of this most unlooked-for event. 'Maggie's happiness is my happiness; and if in hers the chain is broken, which might have fettered my soul in the performance of my vow to aid in crushing this terrible Rebellion, it is my duty cheerfully to submit.'

"And, mamma, what better proof can we have of his truly sincere and noble nature, than is shown in his entire devotedness to Captain Carver, and his pure, unselfish participation in Maggie's joy, that her heart's first love is restored.

"The Captain was overjoyed to see me, and spoke so confidently of being himself soon, under such nurses as Harry, Maggie, and myself, that he has made me as hopeful of his ultimate recovery as he is himself.

"At his request, I told him all that had occurred since we parted in Philadelphia. Harry had already informed him of Frank's imprisonment for saying 'the war was unjust and wholly unnecessary;' and, as I concluded, he drew me down to his side, saying —

"'You have indeed told me a sad, sad tale, and shown me, that even a little hand like this can cripple the wolf, which twice broke into the fold.' Color came into his sunken cheeks, and his eyes were unnaturally bright as he added, 'this state of things cannot last long, for you have Burnside and his "boys" on your soil, Annie. Would to God every State in the Confederacy could say as yours, 'our saviours have crossed the threshold — the portals beyond must unclose at their bidding.'

"What he told me of his last cruise, — he was a captain in the U. S. Navy, — and of his overwhelming surprise and regret on his return, to find his country in a state of civil feud, and no less agreeable news awaiting him on reaching his native State, — that of being numbered among the dead, (a brother-officer of the same name had sickened and died in the tropics,) I have not time to detail now; and so will only repeat the disasters which followed his embarking for active service, South. These are his words: —

"'The ship, in which I sailed from New York, was wrecked off this coast last October, and, with the survivors of another wreck, I was brought to this town. Exposure and subsequent imprisonment brought on fever; but, through the untiring exertions of a Dr. Pill, my own and comrades' sufferings were not only mitigated, but our escape effected on the night preceding the day which was to see us removed to Salisbury. An attack upon this city was then daily expected; and the jailer said, "Old prisoners must be sent off to make room for new ones." I was too weak to be removed far, and, after that first night, was entrusted to the care of a free negro. From the hour of our escape, I have not seen Dr. Pill; and that other friend who occasionally visited the prison, but once, — the day he brought the nurse to my cot, and told her I was a sick man sent up from Beaufort. He promised to pay her well if she did her duty faithfully, and said, on leaving, he should call daily. He never came again.

"'The Provost Marshal had use for the house which we occupied, and had us removed into a dilapidated building in the heart of the city. The removal was made in the midst of a drenching rain, and, taking a severe cold, a relapse of fever followed. For days I was unconscious; once it seemed as if I lay on the battle-field, dying of thirst, so hidden from sight as to escape the observation of the ambulance corps. The flitting of the death-angel, whose icy touch had chilled to endless rest thousands on the same bloody plain, drew near. A vague sensation of some loved presence at my side made me turn from the stern figure bending over me, and I heard a voice which thrilled my inmost being. I knew it, Annie; it was not unlike your own. I was spellbound. Once the voice ceased, and again came the flutter of those dark wings; but the song, which was to me the elixir of life, rose up anew. The delightful trance, which followed, I cannot describe satisfactorily; a beautiful being seemed ever to be leading me on by her bewitching notes, by silvery streams, up beauteous banks, through fields redolent with nature's blooms. On and on we went, she ever turned from me, ever eluding my grasp. By a limpid pool, she lingered a moment, and, in its placid waters, I saw her face reflected. It was my own dear Maggie! I shouted her name; she was gone! only a tiny ripple told me where the wavelets closed over her. I tried to follow, but my feet clung to the ground; then — But no matter, Annie; I was but dreaming. Burnside's guns aroused me; the first peal brought me upright, and there was my own lost Maggie by my side!'

"'How did she discover you?' I asked, burning with impatience to hear the *dénouement*.

"'I could not wait to be found out; I said "Margaret," when she had finished tying up my head, the morning following the Newbern battle.'

"'Oh! what did she say?'

"'Ask her; here she comes,' was the smiling rejoinder; and the glance, which welcomed Maggie to his side, almost made me envious of her happiness.

"I asked Harry about Maggie's imprisonment. He said, 'She never alludes to it, it was fraught with so much suffering to Horace; her faithful servant, Lizzie, had tracked her mistress, and rescued her, Capt. Carver, and several others, from the burning house where they were imprisoned; that he came up with Burnside's army, and met Maggie on the shore road, protecting the almost lifeless body of Ralph Bierce; he was carried to a house near, and nursed by Maggie until he breathed his last; he left papers in her charge for his sister Helen, requesting her to read before delivering them.'

"The Bierce family, Harry thinks, must have left in the panic, and, although letters have been written by several 'flags,' no news, as yet, has come from them. Harry is very confident he shall find them during his sojourn in Secessia.

"I was pleased to hear, in your last letter to me, that Carrie was married to her dear Captain. But what can be Sallie Prue's feelings, now her 'hero' is dead? She, that exacted such a promise from him before he left, to bring her trophies of the enemies; that looks to the days of Indian warfare for example. His sufferings must have been intense. To think of his lying on the battle-field three days and nights, —

and died before reaching the hospital. How sad! She never saw him again after he made that vow to her, that memorable night of the ball.

"Now, mamma, agreeably to my promise, you shall have the particulars of my trip here; every incident, as it transpired, I put upon paper on the spot, and here you have them, strung in as straight a line as the parlor chairs when Lucy 'rights up to order.'

"From Salisbury to Kinston, long faces, dust, and universal commotion at any unusual sound; but no surprise, and Kinston was reached in safety. A delay there of a few days; multitudinous questions asked, and answered or parried as suited us best; at last, came the official announcement: 'The flag was ready, and the ambulance approaching the hotel.'

"With a bounding heart, I bade uncle good by, and sent a kiss back to you, and the dear imprisoned ones.

"Hear now what a novel kind of a vehicle a Secesh ambulance is; a very large milk-cart, minus cans, with seats like an omnibus, made of hard pine, only rendered comfortable by sitting on one's satchel; wheels immense, — just such ones as Noah would have fashioned for his ark, if, on land, it had been ordained to trundle during that long night of merited punishment. I can sincerely say the felicity of rising gently up and falling as quietly down of carriage motion, can never be fully appreciated until one has endured the compound jolting of a springless ambulance wagon on one of our 'particular bad roads,' during the long hours of a day, and not a few of the night also. But all discomfort was swallowed up in the enjoyment afforded me by my travelling companions' grievous complaints of what their folly had brought upon themselves. There were six ladies and myself in the ambulance; and, with the exception of one, from their conversation, I should judge they were on 'their journey home.' Two of them were wives of officers taken in a recent skirmish on the road we were travelling, then on their way to the Yankees, hoping to be allowed to go North to share their husbands' captivity. The other four were in search of effects left behind, and, if permission were granted them, to remain within Federal lines. All were bitter Secessionists, and it is certainly not unbecoming in me to avow that, from my heart, I wished that those whom they so unmercifully reviled, might refuse them every petition they made. Some little idea of their conversation may be gathered from the following, which, if not very courteously worded, was certainly expressive of decidedly ruffled feelings.

(Young lady left behind in the Newbern panic) — "'It is, indeed, too true that the conductor, and not the terrified passengers, who put him up to disobey orders, is the special object of our gallant General's wrath. He has avowed his determination to have him strung up when caught. There is but little fear of his threat being carried into execution, if it happens he is as good at running as our General himself.'

(My neighbor) — "'Why speak so disrespectfully of Gen. Runn? He certainly did all a man could do on that disastrous day. The militia *would run*, and a panic followed.'

(Her *vis-a-vis*) —

"'In all the trade of war, there is no feat
So noble as a brave retreat.'

"'Gen. Runn led this rout in person, and, for the deed so nobly done, his name should be written upon the brightest page of American history!'

(Strange lady)—"'Ladies, you labor under a gross mistake if you attribute the defeat at Newbern, and that most disgraceful rout, to mismanagement on the part of Gen. Runn. He was not, to my certain knowledge, General commanding. Upon Gen. DeLeigh rests the entire responsibility.'

(Lady No. 4) — "'Gen. DeLeigh? No, madam, that cannot be; for, at the time of the battle, he was at Goldsborough, unfit for service.'

(Stranger) — "'Report says he was beastly intoxicated; be that as it may, he was not on the field, although he had orders from the Commander-in-chief to —'

(First speaker, interrupting) — "'That is the way blunders are tossed from shoulder to shoulder. Gen. Runn may be a worthy citizen, and a fair politician, but a *general* he is not!'

(*Vis-a-vis*, with a mocking laugh) — "'There is an aroma about run-down politicians, particularly grateful to the olfactories of our incomparable President.'

(My neighbor) — "'Well, ladies, we are fortunate, and we may congratulate ourselves that we are so, — that affairs for us are no worse. Had the Yankees followed up their successes, Goldsborough, Raleigh, and who doubts but the entire State, would have fallen into their hands; for, so far as I can learn, the late rout extended, not only throughout eastern, but middle Carolina. To whom is such unparalleled cowardice chargeable? Certainly, not to our soldiers, but to the lack of ability, and criminal neglect, of the officers who command them.'

(Stranger, sharply) — " ' If, in your censure, you include Gen. Runn, you malign a character you know nothing of. *He* is fully exonerated from the blame of the late defeat, which was, at first, attached to him. If not convinced of the truth of my assertion, *I*, his sister, have a letter from headquarters, which, on perusal, will satisfy the most prejudiced among you.'

"An unbroken silence followed the speaker's emphatic words; perhaps the ladies felt some compunctions of conscience for their free speech; if so, they expressed none.

"Our escort, consisting of twenty horsemen, were finely mounted; a turn in the road would conceal them from view, and another would fully display the prancing horses and their unarmed riders, the white flag being their only shield from the foe, which one of the ladies declared, in great trepidation, she saw dodging behind the oaks, pines, and alders, which lined the road on either side.

"I knew we were not within Yankee lines, and, although greatly excited myself, as every moment brought us nearer the 'blue-coats,' I laughed immoderately at the fears of the others, when, as was often the case, the escort was quite out of sight; which occasioned the remark, 'I appeared as merry as if on a picnic, instead of approaching a den of robbers and murderers.'

"With night shadows the escort surrounded the ambulance, the flag-bearer keeping a few yards in advance, which occasioned a livelier conversation than had hitherto prevailed. It was, however, startlingly interrupted by a volley of musketry, fearfully near.

"'Halt!' from our Captain followed.

"'We shall go no farther to-night, ladies,' was his remark as he cantered up with his company, after a reconnoisance down the road. 'Our pickets have been driven in by an attacking party, how formidable we cannot ascertain. A short ride farther,' he added, 'would have brought us to a well-furnished but deserted house; unfortunately, the enemy are much nearer than we expected, which circumstance will constrain you to accept such accommodations for the night as the forest alone will afford.'

"The descent from the wagon was slow and painful; some of its occupants shook violently, and the officer's hand which lifted me from my high perch, was, I remarked, exceedingly tremulous.

"Around the bivouac fire we gathered, and although the laugh and jest were forced, they were resorted to as the only means available to curtain from sight the phantom army which the fitful blaze disclosed, now at the right, then at the left of the fear-smitten ones, cowering under the white fluttering ensign, — their only defence. To beguile the long hours of that anxious night, the suggestion 'that the pines should be dressed in white, and that a general illumination should announce to the hovering marauders that the legitimate owners of the soil deigned to hold parley with them,' was heartily acted upon. Soon, huge piles of light-wood blaze lit up far-reaching vistas; and the white drapery which the trunks supplied, floating from bough and pine-top, brought the comforting thought of protecting angels. Intense excitement kept all eyes open, but no alarm sounded; and, at daybreak, 'guardian angels' were packed up, fires stamped out, and flag-bearer, escort, and ambulance formed into line.

"'We have all seen Yankees,' said my neighbor, as the falling back of the horsemen intimated that the prospect was fair those we sought were near.

"'I never have,' I whispered, for, mamma, that term rightly belongs to New Englanders, and I was sure I had never seen any of them. What followed was too low for my ear to catch, except, 'thin lips, infallible sign of cupidity and insensibility; for personal appearance, imagine a shoat playing the dandy, and, with all the egotistical obtrusiveness of the race, knocking one's feet from under if one dares dispute the right of way. The monsters! (spoken more loudly) 'one would demean one's self to look at them; I never will.'

"'Nor I, nor no lady or miss would,' said my *vis-a-vis*, bowing to me.

"'Not less in the physique than in the soldierly bearing of our escort will the comparison hold good. See! yonder they are!' cried Gen. Runn's sister, lifting her finger.

"A bend in the road, and the Yankees were before us! all blue, all fire, all pluck.

"Captain Guier took the flag and advanced to meet the Yankee officer, who had dismounted and was approaching us. I glanced at my companions, and discovered that they were not only *looking* at but returning the bold stare of the foe with haughty insolence. Bright were their faces, dressed 'in anger's flush,' as the consciousness of their humiliating position was thrust home by the self-satisfied smile which shone on the resolute, but awfully bearded faces before us.

"'Pity they could not hide their base deeds, as they do their hateful faces,' was whispered, and many remarks of like nature went round, to which, however, I paid no heed; for I was intent in my scrutiny to find one point of resemblance between the dignified bearing of the Northern officer, who stood head and shoulders above Captain Guier, and the dandy grunter of the ditch.

"'You must wait patiently,' said our gallant Captain, approaching, 'until word comes from Gen. Burnside whether the flag will be received.'

"The delay, which the others pronounced 'insupportable! monstrous!' I spent in watching, with unbounded delight, these men, so hostile to one another under auspices other than the white flag, mingle promiscuously, exchanging papers, and, not infrequently, jokes, which provoked hearty laughter. Again I glanced at my *compagnons du voyage*; each held a book, but their disturbed faces showed that their thoughts wandered. Perhaps the bearing of the victors awoke in them the consciousness of having fanned the blaze which had showered the South with clouds of *blue cinders*, which water could not quench, nor fire nor smoke consume, which perished their broad acres and smothered their homes!

"The flag was accepted! and adieux to our little band followed. Eyes, which brimmed as the white flag fluttered from sight, flashed angrily at the chilling courtesy of the tall captain, who, with a slight movement of his hand, motioned the ladies to enter the carriage in waiting.

"'No egotistical obtrusiveness about that Yankee officer,' I thought; and I laughed inly that Secesh was denied the opportunity of displaying the abhorrence which had been so nicely gotten up for the occasion.

"The officer's authoritative tone and manner reminded me forcibly of the 'there, sit there!' of him of the birchen rod, — a practical illustration of the 'set down' judiciously being omitted.

"The ride was silent and rapid. 'Blue-coats, splendidly mounted, rode boldly; while their horses, elate, doubtless, with the consciousness of the power they bore, bent every sinew in the mad gallop which filled our eyes with dust, and completely settled the fact, that Yankees could ride as well as fight. Mamma, as I looked upon these men, and thought of the resolute boldness and unflinching purpose which armed them to wipe out the foul treachery, which, with the blackness of night, sullied the fairest banner the earth ever hung out, this flighty little heart of mine was awe-smitten; and love and deference unconsciously increased to adoration, as a mishap to our carriage brought these soldiers about us, and, for the first time, I stood with them face to face. Not plainer was the eagle on their buttons than the eagle light in their eyes, flashing the heroic ardor and determination which animates them to achieve their lofty aim, — that of restoring unity and law.

"The damage to the carriage was slight, and Newbern was reached at last. Did those hearts beside me thrill as mine, when the tented field, with the 'Red, white, and blue' sky flower, burst upon our view! that could not be; for those who looked out from canvas homes beneath were enemies! The burst of music which greeted our ears as we drove into the city, must have melted the exiles to contrition, or turned them to stone. What they saw or felt, I can only conjecture; for my heart, overflowing with the full, glorious consciousness that I was free, drowned my eyes in tears.

"I left my letter, last night, to answer Maggie's call to hear the letters which Ralph Bierce wished her to read, and which Harry takes with him to deliver to the family. The contents were mostly of his brother William. Harry will tell you of the efforts of that brave William Bierce to stand firm to his country, to honor the true flag, and how he died. His diary was found upon Ralph's person. On it was written, 'For Nellie; not to be read until North and South are one!'

"Harry interrupts me, crying —

"'No time for adieux! See, the white flag is passing!'

"It is indeed so, and I must not detain him, only to enclose these last unspeakably happy words, — the balm for every watching, aching heart —

"'*Burnside is coming!*'"

CHAPTER XXXVII.

CONCLUSION.

Twilight has deepened into dusk, and, through the open casement, the moon, bright, full, and radiant, falls upon the couch of a dying woman. A fold of cloth covers her face all but her mouth, through which her breath comes intermittent. Two watchers, one on each side, alone are near her in her death agony, — Helen Bierce, and poor sightless Vine.

"Lift me, Vine, and place the cushion at my back; there, that will do; now, Helen, you and Vine take my hands; I cannot see you, but I must feel you, while I utter my last words."

The door opens, and a step is heard. "Is that you, Charles?" and, as the one welcomed by an expressive glance from Helen, drew near, and knelt down, the sufferer resumed —

"You have all been kind to me. No act of mine, but God's mercy, has made you so, and He will reward you, — He, who took from me my sight, but let light into my soul, black with sin, and revealed to me blessed visions of a bright and living world, after night here.

"Tell Francis, Helen, I forgive him; he thought me dead, or nearly so, or he would not have left me as he did, in that terrible panic. It was for my jewels I re-entered the burning house; I got them, but lost all, save this faint spark of life, which soon, now, will expire. The beam fell across my face; Francis tried to lift it, but it was beyond his strength, and he left me to get aid. The Yankees found me; they carried me to the hospital, and cared for me tenderly; they told me my burns were of such a nature that I could not live. The torment, the torture, and agony of those days, found relief at last. A soldier was dying near me; a chaplain daily talked and prayed with him; and, although my stubborn heart at first refused to admit the truths he uttered, it yielded, and finally craved them. I called the chaplain to me; he asked me 'if I ever prayed?' I told him 'no;' he said 'it was time,' and requested me to repeat after him the Lord's Prayer. I did so, and from that moment, all that, which was to me stern and awful in religion, vanished; for the 'peace which passeth all understanding,' was mine.

"You found me, Helen, a burnt and sightless being; you found Vine, also, and removed us here; and, for your devotion to us both, God, who is ever near, will bless you.

"Charles Coxe, I do not ask you how you discovered Helen through her disguise. I do not care to know, so long as I am sensible she has yielded to the voice of truth and passion. My legacy to you both, is Vine,—poor sightless Vine, made so by my hand, and, for which sin, I have passed through a fiery furnace, but found beyond 'the everlasting arms.'

"Vine, be to Helen what, for the last few months, you have been to me. You have been wicked; I made you so, and God has forgiven us both."

The sinking woman's voice failed her; and, as slight spasms passed over her wasted frame, they laid her tenderly down, and, with moist eyes, waited for the final struggle. It came at length. With a convulsive motion of the thin, white hands, and a quiver of the lips, it passed.

An hour later, and Charles and Helen sat at the open window. The soft, calm light, from without, reveals traces of great and recent emotion upon Helen's face, and repeatedly, and fervently, she presses her brother's diary to her lips as if it were, indeed, a sentient thing. Lifting her streaming eyes to the star-lit canopy above her, she breathed —

"Willie, your appeal is not in vain; I *will* ' *do all* to the glory of God.' Heaven grant that my heart, once so cold with pride and self-will, may yield to be directed by a zeal as ardent and enduring as your own."

She ceased to speak, and other thoughts, which she cared not to utter, kept her eyes still bent upon the distant heavens.

A moved, low voice at her side aroused her; and, yielding to the tender caress, which, as his affianced bride, she had no wish to withhold, she murmured —

"Yes, Charley. To-morrow is Maggie's wedding-day. You will see her; then tell her all."

"And my mother!"

Helen turned, and pointing to the dead, said: "Your promise is no longer binding." After a few moments of increasing emotion, she sobbed: "Mother's death has taught me how easy a thing it is to die; but what a frightful thing it is to live, and not rightly!"

"To know the right, and nobly to live up to it, is glorious," Charles said cheerfully: and, wishing to divert her thoughts from the channel of bitter regret, he resumed, laying his hand upon the papers, still in her trembling grasp —

"You do not ask me how I obtained these."

"The satisfaction of having them is complete; there is no room for curiosity;" with something of her former animation in voice and manner, she added, "I saw Harry Blout in the hospital wards to-day; and so overwhelming was my surprise, for I thought him long since dead, that, involuntarily, his name escaped me. He turned towards me, but I had recovered my composure, and, conscious that I was not recognized, I ventured a remark about one of the patients."

To Helen's infinite amazement, her companion related to her Harry's motives for taking the field; his adventures under the assumed name of Dr. Pill, and his long and unavailing search for her and her father's family, while in Secessia: "And, Helen, he returned but yesterday to Newbern, to be present at his Cousin Maggie's wedding. Accompanying him, were several Union friends; among the number he mentioned John McGowan, who, through the influence of powerful partisans, was recently released from imprisonment, — his son Frank, having secured his escape some two months since, from like suffering. One other he alluded to most feelingly,—a Mrs. Weasel, whose husband died in Salisbury; her children are those you have often seen with Maggie Blout. Helen, dear Helen," he added most earnestly, "you must see Harry before the next flag leaves, — for he goes back to remain, he tells me, — and hear the account of his travels through the western part of the State. There, Union men, escaped from desolated homes, jails, and swamps, do congregate, armed with a determination to maintain their rights, which sets, dangers and tyranny at defiance.

And who, think you, is their avowed and devoted leader? Richard Whedden!

"Harry found him, not only restored to sound health, but the enthusiastic admiration of the crowds which throng to hear him. The mighty impulses of his soul have been stirred to achieve mighty ends; and, with his unbounded love for the Federal Government, who that hears him, and knows his courage, intrepidity, and unflinching purpose, can doubt that, to its sovereignty, he will yet gloriously return his adopted State."

"His field is yours, Charley. *There*, duty calls us both."

"Be it so;" and the room, hitherto cold in the moonlight and death-shadows, glows now in the sunshine of ardent hope and lofty patriotism.

www.ingramcontent.com/pod-product-compliance
Lightning Source LLC
Chambersburg PA
CBHW032118230426
43672CB00009B/1782